Jesus' Teachings about MONEY

A Guide to Biblical Stewardship

Loyal E. Golv

Kirk House Publishers
Minneapolis, Minnesota

Dedicated to:

Ruth, John, and **Naomi Golv**
> my on-going mentors

Clint Keay
> whose encouragement brought this book to completion

Leonard Flachman, publisher
> whose insights added new dimensions to this book.

Jesus' Teachings about MONEY
A Guide to Biblical Stewardship
Loyal E. Golv

Copyright 2007 Loyal E. Golv. All rights reserved

ISBN-13: 978-1-933794-09-9
ISBN-10: 1-933794-09-7

Kirk House Publishers, PO Box 390759, Minneapolis, MN 55439
www.kirkhouse.com • publisher@kirkhouse.com
1-888-696-1828

Manufactured in the United States of America

TABLE OF CONTENTS

CHAPTERS	TITLES AND TEXTS	PAGES	— RELATED TEXTS —
[C-1]	Gold for Our King Matthew 2:1-23	1 - 5	JOHN 1:43-51; PHILIPPIANS 2:6-8 JOHN 18:33-42; MATTHEW 27:57-61 REVELATION 21:21
[C-2]	His Forerunner and Ours Matthew 3:1-17, Luke 3:1-20	6 - 10	MARK 1:11; JOHN 1:19-36 MATTHEW 11:2-19; ISAIAH 6:18-19
[C-3]	His Temptation and Ours Matthew 4:1-11	11-14	MARK 1:12-23; LUKE 4:1-13 HEBREWS 4:14; MATTHEW 6:9-13 LUKE 11:2-4
[C-4]	Money and the Making of Disciples Matthew 4:18-22	15-19	MARK 1:16-20; LUKE 5:1-11 JOHN 1:36-42; LUKE 4:38-39
[C-5]	The Teaching of Jesus: At the Beginning Matthew 5:3 and Luke 6:20	20-24	MATTHEW 19:24-26; GENESIS 17:1-2 LUKE 1:68-79; HEBREWS 8:1-13 GENESIS 13:2;
[C-6]	Reconciliation, Then . . . Matthew 5:21-26	25-29	I JOHN 4:16-20; LUKE 15:11-32 ACTS 9:13-18, PHILEMON 1-25
[C-7]	A Special Place for the Poor Matthew 6:1-4	30-34	2 CORINTHIANS 8:2-14; JAMES 2:1-8 ACTS 4:32-5:11; MATTHEW 25:31-40 I TIMOTHY 6:17-19
[C-8]	Treasures: On Earth, In Heaven Matthew 6:19-21	35-39	ECCLESIASTES 2:11; 9:11-12 LUKE 12:13-31; PHILIPPIANS 4:11-19 2 CORINTHIANS 8:9; 11:24-28
[C-9]	The Linchpin: the People of God Matthew 6:24	40-45	EXODUS 20:2-17; EPHESIANS 5:5 LUKE 16:1-13; MATTHEW 26:14-16 MATTHEW 27:3-10; 28:13; ACTS 4:34
[C-10]	The Linchpin: the World of Commerce Matthew 6:24	45-51	MATTHEW 25:14-30; LUKE 19:11-27
[C-11]	Economics and the Kingdom: A Personal Evaluation Matthew 6:25-34	52-56	LUKE 12:22-34; PHILIPPIANS 4:11-12
[C-12]	Economics and the Kingdom: The Broad Scope of History Matthew 6:25-34	57-61	LUKE 12:22-34; MATTHEW 13:45-56 I CORINTHIANS 4:1; I PETER 4:10 EPHESIANS 1:8-10;

CHAPTERS	TITLES AND TEXTS	PAGES	— RELATED TEXTS —
[C-13]	Ministry Without Money Matthew 10:1-15	62-66	MARK 6:7-13; LUKE 9:1-16; 10:1-12 EPHESIANS 6:9-10; PROVERBS 9:7-9 LUKE 22:35
[C-14]	Looking Beyond the Obvious Matthew 13:1-51	67-72	MARK 4:1-34; LUKE 8:1-15 ISAIAH 6:9-10; MATTHEW 21:28-46 JOHN 1:3, 14
[C-15]	Listening at the Edges Matthew 14:13-21 and John 6:1-13	73-77	MARK 6:30-44; LUKE 9:10-17 MATTHEW 15:32-38; JOHN 6:25-71
[C-16]	Life and Language Matthew 16:24-26	78-82	MARK 8:34-37; 8:29-31; 9:2-13 LUKE 9:23-27; 2 PETER 1:16-18 JOHN 14:6
[C-17]	Money and Power Matthew 18:23-35	83-87	MATTHEW 18:15-22; MATTHEW 6:12 GENESIS 39:1-41, 57
[C-18]	Wealth: a Worrisome Wonder Matthew 19:16-26	88-94	MARK 10:17-31; LUKE 18:18-30 ROMANS 3:12; JOHN 1:10, 12, 16 EPHESIANS 2:8-10; ACTS 4:32, 34
[C-19]	Generosity: His and Ours Matthew 20:1-16	95-99	LAMENTATIONS 3:22-223 JOHN 15:1-11
[C-20]	Prayers or Preyers Matthew 21:12-17	100-104	MARK 11:11, 15-19; LUKE 19:45-48 JOHN 2:13-22; MATTHEW 1:1-17, 25 LUKE 3:23-38; JOHN 1:10; LUKE 2:41-51 MATTHEW 17:24-28; ISAIAH 56:7 JEREMIAH 7:11; PSALM 69:9
[C-21]	Taxes and Giving Matthew 22:15-22	105-109	MARK 12:13-17; LUKE 20:20-26 LUKE 23:34; 1 CORINTHIANS 4:12 GALATIANS 2:1, 2, 10 2 CORINTHIANS 8:5; 9:2, 7, 8 1 CORINTHIANS 5:1, 2; 11:17-34 JOHN 3:16-17; LUKE 15:11-
[C-22]	Counting the Cost Luke 10:25-32	110-115	MATTHEW 19:16; MATTHEW 18:20
[C-23]	Money and the Lost Son Luke 15:11-32	116-121	LUKE 15:11-24; LUKE 15:25-32 LUKE 15:3-6; LUKE 15:8, 9
[C-24]	Rich Man, Poor Man Luke 16:19-31	122-126	LUKE 8:1-3; MARK 15:40-41 MATTHEW 19:23-26; 2 CORINTHIANS 8:9-14 JOHN 14:20:24-29; MATTHEW 6:19-21

CHAPTERS	TITLES AND TEXTS	PAGES	— RELATED TEXTS —
[C-25]	Pharisee / Tax Collector / Tithing Luke 18:9-14 and Luke 11:42	127-131	MATTHEW 23:23; ACTS 23-6 ACTS 9:1-19; LUKE 5:27-28 MATTHEW 6:3,4; LUKE 21:1-4 GALATIANS 5:22,23; ACTS 18:1-4 1 CORINTHIANS 16:1-4; PHILIPPIANS 4:15-20
[C-26]	Salvation Now! Luke 19:1-10	132-136	LEVITICUS 6:4-5; MATTHEW 23:23 LUKE 18:25; 2 CORINTHIANS 5:17
[C-27]	Concluding Contrasts Luke 10:38-42 and John 11:1-45	137-141	ACTS 5:33-42; ACTS 22:3 REVELATION 19:16' LUKE 24:1-4 MATTHEW 5:14-16; ROMANS 6:5-12 2 CORINTHIANS 5:17-21; REVELATION 21:1-5
Biblical References		142-143	
Bible Studies		144-150	
Basic Reference Books		151	
Bibliography		152-156	
Index		157-160	

Additional Information

The principal translation used in these chapters is the
    New Revised Standard Version of the Bible,
        The New Oxford Annotated Bible.
The translations used for comparative purposes are the
    Revised Standard Version of the Bible,
        The Oxford Annotated Bible, and the
    Jerusalem Bible, and the
    King James Version of the Bible.

In these chapters, quotations are printed in italics.

    With all due respect for the scholars who evaluate Biblical texts in terms of historical and literary criticism, these chapters focus on the texts primarily in terms of their narrative value.

The Author

Loyal Golv grew up in a large city (Chicago, Illinois) and in a small town (Radcliffe, Iowa). During WWII, the day after graduating from high school, he was inducted into the Navy. His undergraduate degrees were earned at Waldorf College, Forest City, Iowa, and at Northwestern University, Evanston, Illinois. His degrees in theology were earned at Luther Seminary, St. Paul, Minnesota: a B.Th. degree in 1953 and a D.Min. degree in 1978.

For 28 years he was a parish pastor serving congregations located in Wibaux, Montana; Fargo and Wahpeton, North Dakota; Northfield, Minnesota; Brookings, South Dakota; plus interim ministries in Pierre, South Dakota, and Forest City, Iowa. Stewardship was a significant part of his parish ministry.

For ten years prior to retirement, the ministry of stewardship became a full-time opportunity as he served on the national staff of the American Lutheran Church, Minneapolis, and of the Evangelical Lutheran Church in America, Chicago.

His previous writings include *The Cross and Crises,* Augsburg Publishing House, 1961; *Augsburg Sermons,* Augsburg Publishing House, 1975; and *The Catechism and Creative Learning,* his doctoral thesis, 1978.

PREFACE

Jesus spoke about money more frequently than about any other topic except for his central theme, The Kingdom of God. This book collects what Jesus said about money. Confronted by Jesus' humor and enlightened by his wisdom, we find new wisdom for the decisions we make about our money day after day.

This book is good news for busy people. It is a resource book with no beginning and no end. Approaching the ministry of Jesus from a monetary perspective reveals the great variety of his many insights that can enrich our ministries and our lives. That variety has resulted in chapters that are distinctive. To a remarkable degree each chapter stands alone. You may open the book and begin at any chapter.

The focus on the message of Jesus rather than on an author's stewardship agenda makes this a versatile book. For the Bible study leader there are resources to enable the preparation of a single study or a series of studies. For the Christian seeking a new context for daily devotions the book may be read from beginning to end. Stewardship committees seeking biblical themes and program ideas will find that this book opens the Bible to them. Pastors who want to integrate stewardship themes into their sermons will discover an abundance of help here.

The texts for each chapter were selected simply by beginning at the beginning of the New Testament—moving page by page through the Gospel of Matthew, then considering parallel passages in the other Gospels, including texts found only in the Gospel of Luke or the Gospel of John, and finally reaching out to related texts throughout the Bible.

What our Lord taught is echoed in one way or another within other New Testament books. His stewardship teaching informed St. Paul and other apostles. In addition, our Lord's teachings brought to mind passages from the Old Testament. Consequently, this is a summary of New Testament teachings about the ministry of stewardship.

NOTE THE LONG LIST OF BIBLICAL REFERENCES ON PAGES 142 AND 143.

INTRODUCTION

Jesus' Teachings About Money provides insights and encouragement for all Christians for whom money is a worrisome wonder. This book, a *Guide to Biblical Stewardship,* is for the followers of Christ as we earn, spend, save, and share the money entrusted to our care.

Perhaps you are a person whose life is shaped by a scarcity of money. Or, you may be a person whose life is shaped by a surplus of money. Or, over the years, first a scarcity of money and now a surplus of money may have shaped your life.

Money can be embarrassing. Too little money may cause our friends to see only our poverty, not our potential. Too much money may attract new friends who see only our wealth. So, we tend to keep silent about our money.

Money is not funny. Poverty is no joke. Wealth does not prompt the prosperous to see humor in their good fortune. A thoughtful person who grew up in the midst of wealth wrote: "Never in the history of the world have so many people been so rich; never in the history of the world have so many of those same people felt themselves so poor. It is an odd paradox."

It is not the purpose of this book to propose a theory or to preach a sermon. The notes and observations contained on the following pages rose out of my personal life experience.

I was a parish pastor for 28 years. Stewardship was a significant part of my ministry. During the ten-year period prior to retirement, the ministry of stewardship became a full-time opportunity. I traveled around the country, preaching and teaching at various events. Time and again, I shared the simple fact that is noted in the adjacent column.

No one ever asked me the obvious question, "What did Jesus say about money?" If I had been asked, giving a few examples of Jesus' teachings would not have satisfied me nor the person who posed the question.

Retirement provided the opportunity to address the question, to review and wrestle with the teachings of our Lord concerning money. It turned out to be an engrossing and, sometimes, an enervating adventure.

A friend became aware of what I was doing. He asked if he could read the chapters as they were written. As he read he

---

RELATED
NOTES AND OBSERVATIONS

IT SHOULD BE NOTED THAT THE CATEGORY *MIDDLE CLASS* DID NOT EXIST IN THE FIRST CENTURY

LEWIS H. LAPHAM, *MONEY AND CLASS IN AMERICA: NOTES AND OBSERVATIONS ON OUR CIVIL RELIGION,* P. 8

LAPHAM'S FATHER WAS A WEALTHY BUSINESSMAN IN SAN FRANCISCO WHO SERVED FOR A TIME AS THE MAYOR OF THAT CITY.

STUDENTS OF THE NEW TESTAMENT OBSERVE THAT JESUS SPOKE MORE OFTEN ABOUT MONEY THAN ABOUT ANY OTHER TOPIC EXCEPT FOR HIS CENTRAL THEME:
— *THE KINGDOM OF GOD.*

reflected on our Lord's teaching about money from the perspective of a successful businessman. At one point I became stuck. I had nothing more to share with him. I was ready to give up. He would not accept that decision. He had become engrossed in what Jesus taught about money. He wanted to hear the rest of the story, and he hoped that this manuscript would be published. He kept on encouraging me. During the next year, I was finally able to deal with that difficult text.

> IF YOU ENJOY PUZZLES, YOU MAY WANT TO TRY TO DISCOVER WHAT CHAPTER PROVED TO BE SO DIFFICULT

Time and again on this faith journey of study, I became more and more aware of the ways that a book like this would have been of great value to me in my parish ministry.

This is not a work book, but it is a book for Christians working with finances, whether that be personal finances, business finances, or congregational finances. Jesus' teachings are clear: We are called to be good stewards. What is contained in Jesus teachings is not the law, it is an extension of the good news that God gave himself for us.

You may be a person chosen by your congregation to be its president or its treasurer or to serve on the financial board or stewardship board. You will discover that this book becomes a resource to which you can return as you carry out your ministry. The index on pages 158-160 may be a tool you will use.

You may be a person working in the business world. You may be surprised to learn that Jesus spoke about money in ways that are familiar to you. He also spoke of money in ways that will enrich your life.

You may be a person for whom finances are the focus of your profession. Your clients may be persons burdened by a scarcity of money, or they may be burdened by a surplus of money. The teachings of Jesus merit your attention.

You may be a parish pastor for whom the Bible studies on pages 144-151 will be helpful. Those studies may be used as is or, may be shaped by you for presentation to your congregation. The book provides many other resources for Bible studies. You will find much help for integrating stewardship themes into your year-long preaching. The biblical references on pages 142-143 may provide a "quick list" of related passages.

Each chapter is brief. Approaching the relevant texts specifically from a monetary perspective allows the notes and observations the luxury of brevity.

Each chapter provides you three opportunities to encounter Jesus' teachings. The first opportunity is to give attention to the words of Jesus and the commentary provided. The primary purpose of this material is to consider *Jesus' Teachings About Money* as they related to people in the first century and also serve as a guide for us in this 21st century.

The second opportunity, found at the end of each chapter, is to reflect on a portion of your own faith journey against the background of a specific teaching of Jesus. You are encouraged to do what you often do automatically. When you read what Jesus taught and did, ask yourself, "Of what practical value is this for my life, or for the life of my family, now?"

The third opportunity is to review the faith journey of your congregation against the background of what Jesus taught us about money. At the end of each chapter review the specifics of what Jesus taught and did during his ministry. Then, consider a few questions *to* prompt questions of your own related to your congregation's ministries. The notes and observations of your group will provide affirmation for present ministries and, perhaps, suggest some new or revised ministries for your congregation.

Whenever we ponder passages of Scripture from a specific perspective, the Spirit of God takes us on new adventures that often surprise us and bring joy to our lives. At the close of his ministry, Jesus offered a prayer of encouragement for his followers: "Father, . . . now I am coming to you, and I speak these things in the world so that they may have my joy complete in themselves."

Dispelling the darkness created by the love of money, the light of the Gospel will guide you and your congregation as stewards of the gifts entrusted to your care.

Loyal E. Golv
Advent 2007

RELATED NOTES AND OBSERVATIONS

YOU MAY BE A MEMBER OF A GROUP SELECTED FOR THIS PURPOSE.

JOHN 17:13

I TIMOTHY 6:10-12

UNLESS OTHERWISE INDICATED, ALL BIBLICAL QUOTATIONS ARE FROM THE NEW REVISED STANDARD VERSION OF THE BIBLE.

[C-1

GOLD FOR OUR KING

On entering the house, they saw the child with Mary his mother; and they knelt down and paid him homage. Then, opening their treasure chests, they offered him gifts of gold, frankincense, and myrrh.

    Selecting a monetary perspective to review the ministry of Jesus does not mean we lose sight of other vantage points. We could have chosen to review this fascinating story from the perspective of the wise men, or from the vantage point of the other gifts given to Jesus. A quick look at each of these options will help us as we give special attention to the gift of gold.

    Reviewing this story from the perspective of the wise men involves separating this biblical text from the entertaining embellishments acquired over the centuries. The wise men were magi, *non-Jewish religious astrologers who, from astrological observations, inferred the birth of a great Jewish king. . . . Later Christian traditions regard the magi as kings . . . and number them as three (because of the gifts) . . .* This focus prompts us to note that when the wise men arrived in Bethlehem, they saw the child Jesus, not in a manger located in a stable, but *on entering the house.*

    The gifts of frankincense and myrrh were expensive perfumes which served special purposes among the Jews. Frankincense was a symbol of the priestly office. Myrrh was a spice used to anoint a dead body before burial.

    With money as our concern, we focus on the gift of gold. As we give attention to gold against the background of the whole of Scripture, we are taken as far back as the Garden of Eden and as far forward as the New Jerusalem.

    Gold was the currency of kings. It was used for interstate transactions and as gifts given to royalty. Most money in daily use was coined in silver, including the Roman *denarius* and the Greek *drachme*. Sometimes money was simply called *silver*. One parable refers to the *pound*, a translation of the Greek word *mina*, which was worth about three months wages for a laborer. The only Jewish coin mentioned in the New Testament was the *lepton* which was made of copper.

IF YOU SKIPPED OVER THE INTRODUCTION, PLEASE GO BACK AND READ IT NOW.

RELATED NOTES AND OBSERVATIONS

MATTHEW 2:11

CONTEXT:
MATTHEW 2:1-23

THIS STORY IS FOUND ONLY IN THE GOSPEL OF MATTHEW.

THE NEW BIBLE DICTIONARY, P. 765-6

MATTHEW 2:11

EXODUS 30:23-38

JOHN 19:35

GENESIS 2:11-12
REVELATION 21:21

I KINGS 9:10-14
II KINGS 18:14

MATTHEW 26:15

LUKE 19:11-27

Making the judgment that the wise men were scholars, not kings, we wonder how they acquired the gold to give in homage to Jesus, the infant king. Could it be that they shared their scholarly discovery concerning the special star with their own king? Perhaps their king provided the gold together with a royal letter of introduction.

RELATEE
NOTES AND OBSERVATIONS

MATTHEW 2:1-12

When they arrived in Jerusalem and asked, *Where is the child who has been born king of the Jews?*, these Gentile visitors soon gained an audience with King Herod. He took the wise men seriously and later acted on their message with brutal thoroughness.

MATTHEW 2:2

MATTHEW 2:16-18

We remember the hatred of Herod who did his worst to destroy the new born king. We remember how quickly Mary and Joseph had to flee to Egypt to save the life of Jesus. We wonder if, during their exile, the gift of gold became an essential asset which was used to secure the daily necessities of life.

MATTHEW 2:13-15

After the death of Herod in 4 B.C., the holy family was able to return home. In the following years, Jesus, together with his brothers and sisters, grew up in Nazareth. We wonder if Mary told her children about the wise men who paid homage to their oldest brother? Perhaps this story, together with the other events surrounding the birth of Jesus, Mary chose to *treasure* silently *and ponder them in her heart.*

JESUS' BIRTH, ABOUT 6 B.C..

MATTHEW 2:19-23

MATTHEW 13:55-56

JOHN 7:1-9, MATTHEW 12:46-50

LUKE 2:19

At the beginning of his ministry, the kingship of Jesus was openly recognized. As Jesus was gathering his disciples, it was the humor of our Lord which prompted Nathaniel to proclaim, *You are the king of Israel!*

JOHN 1:49

Nathaniel had given voice to the kind of humor that hurts: *Can anything good come out of Nazareth?* This was a common, caustic appraisal for Nazareth was regarded as a backward village. Jesus gave voice to the kind of humor that heals as he said to Nathaniel, *Here is truly an Israelite in whom there is no deceit!*

JOHN 1:45-51
NATHANIEL MAY BE ANOTHER NAME FOR THE DISCIPLE CALLED BARTHOLOMEW;
MATTHEW 10:3

Nathaniel would be quick to see the humor here for he was well acquainted with the story of Jacob, a deceitful man in ancient times who wrestled with God and received the name, Israel. Through this brief conversation, Nathaniel heard our Lord's gracious humor which has within it the power of reconciliation. He responded enthusiastically, *Rabbi, you are the Son of God. You are the King of Israel!*

GENESIS 27:1—32:32

JOHN 1:49

During his earthly ministry, while never denying his kingship, Jesus *did not count equality with God a thing to be grasped, but emptied himself, taking the form of a servant, being born in the likeness of men. And being found in human form he humbled himself and became obedient unto death, even death on a cross.*

PHILIPPIANS 2:6-8

When he stood before Pilate, Jesus was asked point-blank, *Are you the king of the Jews?* A bit later in this interrogation, Jesus explained, *My kingship is not of this world.* Pilate replied, *So you are a king?* Jesus responded, *You say that I am a king. For this I was born, and for this I have come into the world, to bear witness to the truth. Everyone who is of the truth hears my voice.* Pilate then posed the question which multitudes continue to ponder, *What is truth?*

JOHN 18:33-38

When Jesus was crucified, Pilate *had an inscription written and put on the cross. It read "Jesus of Nazareth, the King of the Jews."* When the chief priests complained bitterly and asked him to change the wording of this title, Pilate replied, *What I have written I have written.*

JOHN 19:17-22

Following the death of Christ, two men, secret disciples whose names we know, gave homage to him in their own special ways. Receiving permission from Pilate, Joseph of Arimathea removed the body of Jesus from the cross. Nicodemus, *who had at first come to Jesus by night, also came, bringing a mixture of myrrh and aloes, weighing about a hundred pounds. They took the body of Jesus and wrapped it with the spices in linen cloths, according to the burial custom of the Jews.*

MATTHEW 27:57-58
JOHN 3:1-21

JOHN 19:38-42

They placed the body in Joseph's new tomb *hewn in the rock,* located in a garden near where Jesus had been crucified. Joseph *then rolled a great stone to the door of the tomb and went away. Mary Magdalene and the other Mary were there, sitting opposite the tomb.*

MATTHEW 27:58-61

The gold given to the infant Jesus introduced us to Christ the King and led us on a journey through his life and to his death. The wise men, whose names we do not know, knelt in homage before the new-born King. Hate-filled Herod feared this infant King and tried to destroy him. Humor helped Nathaniel to recognize Jesus as his King. Pilate was puzzled yet he insisted on proclaiming Jesus the King of the Jews.

RELATED NOTES AND OBSERVATIONS

In this story, the gold itself quickly loses its place of prominence. It had served its function in providing an appropriate gift to proclaim a great truth. The ultimate truth is that all the titles and gifts given to Christ our King point to a divine reality beyond the power of human language to encompass.

Setting great words to magnificent music allows us to increase the boundaries of human speech. There comes to mind the unforgettable climax to Handel's *Messiah*. The words are repeated again and again as the choir sings with great power —
King of Kings and Lord of Lords,
and he shall reign for ever and ever.
Hallelujah, Hallelujah, Hallelujah.
Against this background, gold is seen as of secondary importance, scarcely worth mentioning at all.

[C-1]   GOLD FOR OUR KING

Personal Notes and Observations
against the background of the gold given to the infant Jesus and the flight of his family to Egypt.

A few questions to prompt questions of your own related to your faith journey.

When you were young were your parents confronted by a scarcity or money or a surplus of money?

When you were young were your parents confronted by a crisis which tested their faith?

Did their experiences have a positive or a negative effect on your faith journey?

RELATED NOTES AND OBSERVATIONS

THE *RIGHT* WAY TO TAKE ADVANTAGE OF THIS OPPORTUNITY IS TO APPROACH IT IN A WAY WHICH SEEMS *RIGHT* TO YOU.

YOU MAY DECIDE TO READ ALL THE CHAPTERS BEFORE JOTTING DOWN YOUR NOTES RELATED TO EACH CHAPTER;
— OR YOU MAY DECIDE TO JOT DOWN YOUR NOTES IMMEDIATELY AFTER READING EACH CHAPTER.

DO YOU WANT TO JOT DOWN YOUR NOTES IN A JOURNAL?
— OR INTO A COMPUTER FILE,
— OR TO RECORD THEM ON A VOICE TAPE,
— OR ARE YOU CONFIDENT THAT YOU CAN RETAIN YOUR THEM IN YOUR MEMORY?

===

[C-1]   GOLD FOR OUR KING

Congregational Notes and Observations
against the background of the gold given to the infant Jesus and the flight of his family to Egypt.

A few questions to prompt questions of your own related to your congregation's ministries.

During the early years of your congregation was it confronted by a scarcity of money or a surplus of money?

During those early years was your congregation confronted by a crisis which tested their faith?

Did your congregation's experiences have a positive or a negative effect on its faith journey?

(If your congregation has a long history, your group may want to interview a person familiar with that history.)

THE *RIGHT WAY* FOR YOUR GROUP TO TAKE ADVANTAGE OF THIS OPPORTUNITY IS TO APPROACH IT IN A WAY WHICH SEEMS *RIGHT* TO YOU.

WHEN YOU MEET TOGETHER A NUMBER OF QUESTIONS MAY CONFRONT YOU:
— DO YOU WANT TO JOT DOWN YOUR NOTES AFTER READING EACH CHAPTER FOR THE FIRST TIME?
— HOW MANY CHAPTERS DO YOU WANT TO READ BEFORE SHARING YOUR THOUGHTS WITH YOUR GROUP?
— DO YOU WANT A SECRETARY TO RECORD YOUR NOTES AND OBSERVATIONS AT EACH MEETING OF YOUR GROUP?

[C-2]

HIS FORERUNNER AND OURS

RELATED NOTES AND OBSERVATIONS

John (the Baptist) said to the crowds, ... Whoever has two coats must share with anyone who has none ... To tax collectors ... Collect no more than the amount prescribed ... To soldiers ... Do not extort money from anyone ...

LUKE 3:10-14
CONTEXT: LUKE 3:1-22

SEE ALSO: MATTHEW 3:1-17
MARK 1:1-11
JOHN 1:19-36

John the Baptist was the forerunner of Christ. His purpose was to prepare the way for the ministry of Jesus. As we view John's ministry from the perspective of money, we see him as an important forerunner for us, too.

His importance as the forerunner of Christ is underlined in each of the Gospels in differing ways.

- Luke notes that the Baptist's ministry began *in the fifteenth year of the reign of Emperor Tiberias.*

LUKE 3:1

- John writes about the top religious authorities in Jerusalem who wanted him to answer the question, *Who are you?*

JOHN 1:19-23

- Mark begins his Gospel with the ministry of the this great prophet.

MARK 1:1-4

- Matthew points out that his theme is the same theme on which Jesus preached throughout his ministry; *the Kingdom of God.*

MATTHEW 3:2

Jesus saw John the Baptist as *more than a prophet,* indeed, *that among those born of women, no one is greater than John.* We are amazed when Jesus goes on to say, *the least in the kingdom of God is greater than he.* What John teaches concerning money remains of fundamental importance for he prepares the way for our Lord's remarkably new teachings concerning money.

MATTHEW 11:9, 11
CONTEXT:
MATTHEW 11:2-19
SEE ALSO:
LUKE 7:18-29; 16:16.

Unlike our lack of knowledge concerning the wise men, we know a lot about John the Baptist. We know who his parents were, how he received his name, and the ministry for which he was chosen before he was born. However, between his infancy and the beginning of his ministry, very little about his life is revealed in the Biblical record.

HIS PARENTS WERE ZECHARIAH AND ELIZABETH: LUKE 1:5-15.
HOW HE RECEIVED HIS NAME, LUKE 1:57-66.
JOHN'S MINISTRY IS MADE KNOWN: LUKE 1:14-17.
BETWEEN HIS INFANCY AND HIS ADULT LIFE, ONLY LUKE:1:80.

In terms of his appearance and lifestyle, this mighty prophet provides an extraordinary example of a truth about which we continue to sing, *'Tis a gift to be simple, 'Tis a gift to be free.* His words continue to resonate through every segment of society, prompting multiudes of people of honorable intent to ex

JOHN WORE A GARMENT OF CAMEL'S HAIR, A LEATHER GIRDLE AROUND HIS WAIST; HIS FOOD WAS LOCUSTS AND WILD HONEY.

AN OLD SHAKER HYMN.

exercise responsible citizenship for the sake of the common good.

He called the people to repentance, that is, not simply to be sorry for their shortcomings but to change the moral direction of their living. He insisted that they *bear fruit worthy of repentance,* which means to share, in serious measure, their food and clothing with the poor, and to practice their professions with fiscal integrity.

In those days and down through the centuries, the teachings of John the Baptist have been heard as radical and revolutionary. He taught that sharing food and clothing with the poor was not a charitable act worthy of high praise but evidence of an appropriate way of life on the part of the giver.

Tax collectors and soldiers were examples of persons in professions within the realm of public trust. They were not to abuse their power, as was their custom according to this prophet, but rather to be *satisfied with their wages.*

As we reflect on these things, it is easy to bring to mind any number of current examples of the abuse of public trust and of callous indifference toward the poor by persons in positions of power. With a sense of history, we may conclude that this has always been true, and, perhaps, it was more flagrantly true in the past than in the present. It is important to note that the teachings of John the Baptist are being heard and practiced in our time to a degree that may not be widely known nor acknowledged.

Peter Drucker has been an analytical observer of the economic scene for the better part of the 20th century. In a recent book he notes that in America there are now almost one million non-profit organizations active in the public sector. He writes, *The non-profits have become America's biggest employer. Every other American adult (90 million people in all) works at least three hours a week as "unpaid staff", that is, as volunteers for . . . churches and hospitals, for health care agencies, . . .* for community services of all kinds.

For this chapter, it is profitable for us to reflect on the many and various ways our congregations are involved for the sake of the poor. It may be necessary to do some digging to discover the specific ways in which social agencies which receive our support are providing significant help for the poor.

RELATED NOTES AND OBSERVATIONS

LUKE 3:10-14

LUKE 3:14

WITH MORE THAN TWO DOZEN BOOKS PUBLISHED OVER A SPAN OF MORE THAN 50 YEARS, THIS BOOK WAS WRITTEN WHEN HE WAS 83.

POST-CAPITALIST SOCIETY, PETER F. DRUCKER P. 175-176

THE FLOW OF MONEY FROM FAMILIES THROUGH THEIR CONGREGATIONS THROUGH SOCIAL SERVICE AGENCIES TO THE POOR

We may need to reflect on how our financial gifts function as seed money which grows in remarkable ways through the efforts of a great number of paid and unpaid staff, and also as seed money to secure financial grants from a variety of sources.

> RELATED NOTES AND OBSERVATIONS
>
> IS A WAY TO HEED JESUS' TEACHINGS IN MATTHEW 6:2-4.

In a time when it is tempting to hear only the loud voices of cynics and skeptics, it is important for us to watch intently and listen quietly for evidence and indications of public officials and business leaders who do, indeed, live with personal integrity and with deep concern for the welfare of the less fortunate in our land, and in our world.

People of good will, both within and outside of religious groupings, reflect the teachings of John the Baptist by their attitudes and actions. Some of them may never have known that he was their ancient mentor.

It is important, of course, to keep a human face on this awesome prophet. He was such a powerful preacher the whole nation turned out to hear him. They were ready to proclaim him as the promised Messiah or the prophet Elijah returning to this earth. John made it clear that he was simply the *voice of one crying out in the wilderness, "Make straight the way of the Lord."*

> JOHN 1:19-28
>
> JOHN 1:23

When Jesus began his ministry, it became apparent to John that Jesus' teachings went far beyond his own. Languishing in prison for his bold denounciation of Herod, John openly expressed his doubts about Jesus. With patience and compassion, Jesus reviewed for John the social concerns of his miraculous ministry, and then went on to remind the people of the greatness of this prophet.

> MATTHEW 11:2-6
>
> LUKE 7:18-20
> COMPARE THE ANSWER OF JESUS TO JOHN THE BAPIST WITH ISAIAH 29:18-19

Like John the Baptist, doubt remains a painful part of our own faith journey. Even the news that so many millions of adults are serving as volunteers is tempered by the fact that only a small percentage of them are motivated to devote a significant amount of their time and talents in areas where the needs are the most critical.

John the Baptist was our forerunner, too. When we contribute time and effort and financial resources for the sake of the poor, we make some interesting discoveries. As we give of ourselves, we see ourselves within the faces of the poor. What we give in terms of food and clothing or money lifts our own spirits.

> DRUCKER INDICATES THAT AS WE MOVE INTO THE 21ST CENTURY, SOCIAL SERVICE AGENCIES WILL NEED ABOUT 120 MILLION VOLUNTEERS WORKING 5 HOURS EACH WEEK.
> P. 76
>
> L

As we contribute our time and talents, our own lives find greater fulfillment, What we thought would be a sacrifice becomes a source of deep satisfaction.

As our forerunner, this great prophet opens a door of opportunity for us to explore the teachings of our Lord concerning money. As we walk through that door, we are confident that some surprising discoveries can be made which we will treasure as *good stewards of the manifold grace of God.*

RELATED
NOTES AND OBSERVATIONS

I PETER 4:10

[C-2] HIS FORERUNNER AND OURS RELATED NOTES AND OBSERVATIONS

Personal Notes and Observations
    with reference to your forerunner's insights
    about repentance and the appropriate
    way of life for a believer.

A few questions to prompt questions of your own related to your faith journey.

During your faith journey what action did you choose to take to *bear fruit worthy of repentance?*　　　LUKE 3:8

In this 21st century what sins are so commonplace that simply saying we are sorry is accepted as adequate?

As a volunteer within and outside the church, how much time do you give each week for these purposes?

How have these efforts proven to be of value for your faith journey?

==

[C-2] HIS FORERUNNER AND OURS

Congregational Notes and Observations
    with reference to our forerunner's insights
    about repentance and the appropriate
    way of life for a believer.

A few questions to prompt questions of your own related to your congregation's ministries.

Are members of your congregation expected to *bear fruit worthy of repentance?*　　　LUKE 3:8

What opportunities are given to members to share clothing and food to the poor?

In what ways does money flowing through your congregation benefit the poor?

IF A GROUP HAS NOT BEEN SELECTED TO REVIEW THE FAITH JOURNEY OF YOUR CONGREGATION, YOU MAY CHOOSE TO ACCEPT THIS OPPORTUNITY AND TO SHARE THIS EXPERIENCE WITH YOUR PASTOR.

[C-3]

HIS TEMPTATION AND OURS

RELATED
NOTES AND OBSERVATIONS

Again, the devil took him (Jesus) to a very high mountain and showed him all the kingdoms of the world and their splendor; and he said to him, "All these I will give you, if you will fall down and worship me."

MATTHEW 4:8-9

CONTEXT: MATTHEW 4:1-11
SEE ALSO: MARK 1:12-13
LUKE 4:1-13

We are taking this journey through the Gospels from the perspective of money. As we reflect on the temptations of Jesus, we are reminded of another perspective from which we routinely view the writings of Scripture. When we read what has been written, we ask the question, "What does all this mean for us now?"

It is easy for us to relate to the temptations of Jesus. We know what it means to be tempted, and, not the least, to be tempted in relation to money. Money has pervasive power within every part of our day by day living. Our attitudes and actions pertaining to money become defining moments for us.

Battles with temptations are solitary experiences. When we lose these battles, other people's lives may be effected, and they become aware of our failure and our shame. When we win these battles, our lives are shaped in positive ways, but no one may ever know the struggles we endured.

The temptations of Jesus were solitary experiences. No one was with him to take notes on which the Gospel record could be based. Apparently, at some point in his ministry, Jesus shared with his disciples the battles he had fought. He used pictoral language to convey spiritual realities. It is important to know that his life was not free from the temptations which are common experiences for us all.

HEBREWS 4:15

It does not surprise us that each of the three records of this event are different. It is difficult to convey even to our closest friends the inner battles we have endured. It is equally difficult for them to hear us when our soul is laid bare before them. Each of the evangelists describe the temptations of Jesus in their own unique way.

The Gospel of Mark is noted for its brevity. Mark moves quickly from one event to another. *Immediately* is one of his favorite words. The temptations of Jesus are summarized in just two verses: *And the Spirit immediately drove him out into the wilderness. He was in the wilderness forty days, tempted by Satan; and he was with the wild beasts; and the angels waited on him.*

MARK 1:12-13

The metaphor he used to describe this series of temptations was *he was with the wild beasts*. As we reflect on our own temptation experiences, we may relate to that picture of great personal danger and the potential destruction of our moral fiber.

In the Gospels of Matthew and Luke the temptations are listed in a different order, and there are differing details, but the basic content is the same. From the perspective of money, our focus in this chapter is on the metaphorical mountain from which the devil showed Jesus *all the kingdoms of the world and their splendor.*

MATTHEW 4:1-11

LUKE 4:1-13

Satan promised to give Jesus all the wealth and power and glory accorded to the supreme ruler of all earthly kingdoms. Temptations have no power if they are not appealing. Jesus may have remembered his mother telling him about the wise men who hailed him as a new King. He knew his disciples wanted him to become their King. His countrymen believed that when the Messiah came, he would restore for their nation the splendor and independence that was theirs during the reign of King David. How appealing it must have been to contemplate a crown instead of a cross!

MATTHEW 20:20-28

SOME SCHOLARS WONDER IF JUDAS BETRAYED JESUS TO FORCE HIM TO ASSERT HIS KINGLY POWER AND AUTHORITY.

MATTHEW 4:9

All this the devil promised Jesus *if you will fall down and worship me*. Temptations come with a hook. If only we will compromise our integrity this one time, we will be on easy street. If only we will spin the truth this one time; if only we will look the other way this one time; if only . . . if only . . . this one time.

Jesus does not suggest that "the good life" involving money and power and splendor is evil. He did not even question Satan's ability to deliver *all the kingdoms of the world*. Jesus' response went to the heart of this temptation: *Away with you, Satan! For it is written, "Worship the Lord your God, and serve only him."*

MATTHEW 4:8

MATTHEW 4:10

One of the differing details in the Gospel of Luke is found in the concluding verse: *When the devil had finished every test, he departed from him until an opportune time.* For our Lord, as is true for all of us, temptations come throughout our lives. *An opportune time* for the devil is when we, for one reason or another, are particularly vulnerable.

Out in the wilderness, *with the wild beasts,* Jesus was particularly vulnerable. The exhausting struggle which our Lord endured is underscored in this concluding verse in Matthew: *Then the devil left him, and suddenly angels came and waited on him.* This was, indeed, a defining moment in the ministry of Jesus.

To deny the possibility that our Lord could have yielded to temptation is to deny the humanity of Jesus. Winning this lonely battle provided for him the freedom to complete his ministry faithfully and become our Savior.

It is important for us to evaluate this event from the vantage point of the question, "What does this all mean for us now?" Living today in the history of mankind makes this particular temptation of Christ very personal. That our time is unique becomes apparent whenever we pause to reflect on our money. On the one hand, we are confronted by this sad truth: *Mammon is the god of America's civil religion.* Money has not always been a top priority for people in every age.

On the other hand, printed clearly on our money is the motto of our nation, *In God We Trust.* Our trust in God requires a system of values which puts money into its proper place as of SECONDARY importance.

This journey through the New Testament provides an opportunity to reflect on those values which are of primary importance. Equally important, this journey will affirm the secondary IMPORTANCE of money.

Our own journey of faith, and the ministry of our own congregation, can be enlightened by the ministry of Jesus as it is viewed from the perspective of money. His stories can help us see our stories in new ways.

RELATED NOTES AND OBSERVATIONS

LUKE 4:13

MATTHEW 4:11

FOR AN APOCALYTIC PORTRAYAL OF THE BATTLE AGAINST SATAN SEE REVELATION 12:1-17

LESTER THUROW IN *THE FUTURE OF CAPITALISM,* P. 12-16, POINTS TO THE ANCIENT EGYPTIANS, THE ROMAN EMPIRE, AND 15TH CENTURY CHINA AS ILLUSTRATIONS OF SOCIETIES WHERE THE PURSUIT OF MONEY DID NOT HAVE A HIGH PRIORITY.

CONGRESS MADE THIS PHRASE THE OFFICIAL MOTTO OF OUR COUNTRY IN 1956.
WORLD BOOK ENCYCLOPIA, 2001 STANDARD EDITION.

TO TRUST IN GOD IS TO THINK SERIOUSLY ABOUT MONEY AND ITS POWER TO MOLD OUR MINDS FOR GOOD OR FOR ILL.

PERSONAL PIETY IS NOT ENHANCED BY TRYING TO PUT MONEY OUT OF OUR MINDS.

| | | RELATED |
| | | NOTES AND OBSERVATIONS |

[C-3]   HIS TEMPTATIONS AND OURS

Personal Notes and Observations
which are brought to mind by our Lord's battle
against temptation involving money.

*A few questions to prompt questions of your own
related to your faith journey.*

In your judgment, which temptations concerning money are the most appealing in our time?

In your experience, how can one's faith make it possible to win these inner battles with temptation?

No one wins all of these battles. How can our faith bring us back on a path that is *good and acceptable and perfect?*

ROMANS 12:2

OBVIOUSLY, MANY TEMPTATIONS DO NOT INVOLVE MONEY. YOUR REFLECTIONS NEED NOT BE LIMITED TO MONETARY CONSIDERATIONS.

===

[C-3]   HIS TEMPTATIONS AND OURS

Congregational Notes and Observations
which are brought to mind by our Lord's battle
against temptation involving money.

*A few questions to prompt questions of your own
related to your congregation's ministries.*

Within your congregation, are there occasions when members may be particularly vulnerable to monetary temptations?

Are there ways, methods, or procedures which can make members less vulnerable to monetary temptations?

Would periodically paying for professional audits of your congregation's financial records be a way of making you aware of the strengths and weaknesses of the procedures you have been following?

THE BEST TIME FOR A CONGREGATION TO CONSIDER IMPLEMENTING SOME OF THESE CHANGES IS WHEN THERE IS NO REASON TO BE CONCERNED ABOUT FINANCIAL MISCONDUCT.

MONEY AND THE MAKING OF DISCIPLES

And he (Jesus) said to them, "Follow me, and I will make you fish for people." Immediately they left their nets and followed him.

MATTHEW 4:19-20

CONTEXT: MATTHEW 4:18-22
SEE ALSO: MARK 1:16-20
LUKE 5:1-11

As we turn our attention to the disciples of our Lord and to our own discipleship, the perspective of money raises its own special concerns. Monetary considerations prompt us to go in search for meaning.

This chapter allows us to reflect on these monetary matters against the background of a fundamental truth about ourselves. We live in two worlds as did the disciples. Living in two worlds is one of the definitions of what it means to be human. Money means different things in each of these worlds.

We describe these two worlds in various ways. We speak of an inner world and an outer world. We see ourselves within our physical world and in our spiritual world. We come to terms with the world of our mind and the world of our emotions. We turn our attention to the world of things and to the world of relationships. In this chapter we reflect on the meaning of money in both of these worlds.

JACOB NEEDLEMAN WRITES INCISIVELY ABOUT THESE TWO WORLDS IN HIS BOOK, *MONEY AND THE MEANING OF LIFE*, P. 43-72

These two worlds reside so closely within us, disease in one prompts dis-ease in the other, and they share moments of delight. When we neglect one of these worlds, both are impoverished. As we invest time and talent and thoughtfulness in both of these worlds, our lives are enriched.

Now we focus our attention on those very ordinary and highly extraordinary men who followed Jesus and, together with other apostles, were accused of *turning the world upside down*. The calling of Peter, Andrew, James and John is described with abrupt brevity in both Matthew and Mark.

ACTS 17:6

The Gospel of Luke, fortunately, provides a more detailed picture. It begins by describing the scene differently. Matthew and Mark state that Peter and Andrew were *casting their net into the sea*, while James and John were *mending their nets*. Luke indicates that Jesus *saw two boats there on the shore of the lake; the fishermen had gone out of them and were washing their nets.*

MATTHEW 4:18, MARK 1:16

MATTHEW 4:21, MARK 1:19

LUKE 5:2

Of greater importance than these differing details, the three Gospels remind us that the disciples were called to follow Jesus, not during a worship service at the synagogue, nor within the context of a pilgrimage to the temple in Jerusalem, but on a very ordinary day while they were at work earning their money.

In the outer, physical world involving things, we are often identified with reference to the work we do. There may be times when we define ourselves primarily in terms of how we earn a living, perhaps with a subtle emphasis on how much money we make. When we do so, we make ourselves too small. Our Lord came to his disciples and opened their eyes to see new dimensions pertaining to their work.

We are told that Jesus got into one of the boats and asked Peter to put it out a little way from the shore. Then Jesus taught *the crowd from the boat.* We are not told what he said to them but only what he did after he finished speaking. He asked Peter to *"Put out into the deep water and let down your nets for a catch."*

We can almost hear the exasperation in Peter's voice as he replied, *"Master, we have worked all night long but have caught nothing. Yet if you say so, I will let down the nets."* Then this disappointing day at work became fantastic! They caught so many fish, their nets were beginning to break. They filled, not only their own boat, but had to call their partners, James and John, to bring their boat. Both boats were filled so that *they began to sink.*

It would be expected that these fishermen would be filled with jubilation at their great good fortune. For them, two boatloads of fish would be seen in terms of ready cash. After working for nothing throughout the night, now, against all odds, they were confronted with a lot of money.

But, we live in two worlds. Peter, who had counseled against further fishing, was embarrassed and afraid. Within himself he quickly moved from the world of things into the world of relationships. In this world, he saw himself as altogether unworthy to be in the presence of Jesus. *He fell down at Jesus' knees, saying, "Go away from me, Lord, for I am a sinful man!"*

RELATED NOTES AND OBSERVATIONS

LUKE 5:3

LUKE 5:4

LUKE 5:5

LUKE 5:7

IT IS INTERESTING TO COMPARE THIS STORY WITH A SIMILAR EVENT RECORDED IN JOHN 21:3-19.

LUKE 5:8

This had become a highly personal encounter between Peter and his Lord. The crowd which had gathered to hear the teachings of Jesus faded into the background. Some of them may have headed for home, eager to share the news of how lucky those fishermen were to catch so many fish. Peter saw something far greater than luck and far more important than an unmerited monetary gift.

At the center of this event was the supernatural power which Jesus had revealed to Peter and Andrew. Together with their Lord, they were some distance from the shore in *deep water*. The remaining crowd was too far away to see or hear what was happening. At this moment, our Lord revealed his inner self to these disciples.

LUKE 5:4

In the world of things, Jesus had given to these fishermen a gift which they could measure in monetary terms. In the world of relationships, Jesus gave them a far greater gift as he said to Peter, and including Andrew, James and John, *"Do not be afraid; for from now on you will be catching people."* With this gift, the primary focus for their working lives would take on eternal dimensions.

LUKE 5:10

The drama here is captured by the variant readings in the three Gospels.

In Matthew and Mark, concerning Peter and Andrew, we are told, *Immediately they left their nets and followed him.* With reference to James and John, we read, *Immediately, they left their boat and their father, and followed him.* Mark also states that *the hired men* remained behind. Luke concludes this story with these words, *and they left everything and followed him.*

MATTHEW 4:20, MARK 1:18

MATTHEW 4:22, MARK 1:20

LUKE 5:11

How are we to interpret what it meant for them to *immediately* leave *everything*?

The Gospel of John informs us that Andrew had been a disciple of John the Baptist. Andrew and an unnamed disciple of this prophet were with him when he pointed out Jesus as the *Lamb of God.* Andrew and this unnamed disciple who may have been John, the brother of James, followed Jesus in order to speak to him.

JOHN 1:36

JOHN WAS RETICENT TO NAME HIMSELF IN THE GOSPEL WHICH BEARS HIS NAME.

After their conversation, Andrew went and told his brother, Simon, *"We have found the Messiah,"* and brought him to Jesus. Jesus looked at Simon and said to him, *"You are Simon, son of John. You are to be called Cephas" (which is translated Peter).*

So, *immediately,* following their SECOND encounter with Jesus, Peter, Andrew, James and John followed him. To do so, they left *everything*, that is, a fishing business in which they were partners, the father of James and John and their hired men, plus two boatloads of fish waiting to be turned into money. Further, Peter was a married man who left behind his wife and her mother who lived with them.

In this context, *immediately* marks the clear division between the past and future lives of the disciples. Their first priority for the coming days was to follow the Messiah.

Zebedee, the father of James and John, together with the hired men, would take charge of the fishing business. They would sell the boatloads of fish and be faithful stewards of the money received. Peter's wife and her mother would be supported in his absence. *Everything* was left behind, yet *everything* would be cared for in good order.

A new life was beginning for them. Over the coming weeks and months, the disciples would learn from their Lord how to *fish for people*. As we follow in their footsteps, we will also discover what they learned about money and its proper place in this kind of fishing.

RELATED NOTES AND OBSERVATIONS

JOHN 1:40-41

JOHN 1:42

LUKE 4:38-39

[C-4]   MONEY AND THE MAKING OF DISCIPLES

Personal Notes and Observations
    pertaining to the two worlds in which we live.

*A few questions to prompt questions of your own
related to your faith journey?*

As a follower of Christ in the world of things, how is your money used most effectively?

As a follower of Christ in the world of relationships, how is your money used most effectively?

In both worlds, do you see the use of your money as a reflection of your faith?

RELATED NOTES AND OBSERVATIONS

FACING THESE QUESTIONS DOES NOT MEAN THAT WE PUT OURSELVES DOWN.

FACING THESE QUESTIONS CAN STRENGTHEN OUR FAITH JOURNEY ON THE ROAD TO ABUNDANT LIVING.

===

[C-4] MONEY AND THE MAKING OF DISCIPLES

Congregational Notes and Observations
    in response to turning members into disciples.

*A few questions to prompt questions of your own
related to your congregation's ministries.*

Within your congregation does your ministry to members differ from your ministry to disciples?

When members discover their calling to be disciples, what new meaning does money have for them?

Within your congregation what is the meaning of money, and how it this meaning made known?

THE GOAL IS NOT TO CONFUSE YOU, OR TO PUT DOWN YOUR CONGREGATION.

THE GOAL IS TO STRENGTHEN THE MINISTRIES OF YOUR CONGREGATION.

THE TEACHINGS OF JESUS:

AT THE BEGINNING

RELATED
NOTES AND OBSERVATIONS

Blessed are the poor in spirit, for theirs is the kingdom of heaven.

MATTHEW 5:3
CONTEXT:
    MATTHEW 5:1—7:28

Blessed are you who are poor, for yours is the kingdom of God.

LUKE 6:20
CONTEXT: LUKE 6:17 — 7:1

    As we begin these chapters on the teachings of Jesus from the perspective of money, we are immediately struck by the complexity of its simplicity. Teachings as simple and straightforward as the beatitudes quickly invite us to probe into them more deeply.

    The first beatitude from the Sermon on the Mount speaks about the *poor in spirit*. The same beatitude from the Sermon on the Plain is directed to *you who are poor*. If we are to deal with the complexities of our own lives, both versions of this beatitude become important for us.

WHEN JESUS SAW THE CROWDS, HE WENT UP THE MOUNTAIN....
MATTHEW 5:1
HE CAME DOWN WITH THEM AND STOOD ON A LEVEL PLACE...
LUKE 6:17

    The first version deals with spiritual poverty. We lack the spiritual resources to earn our way into the kingdom. The second version is directed toward those who are financially poor. If we are not in that category, will our money keep us out of the kingdom? What does it mean to be poor? What does it mean to be rich?

MATTHEW'S VERSION, USUALLY BUT NOT ALWAYS, SPEAKS OF THE *KINGDOM OF HEAVEN*. LUKE'S VERSION SPEAKS OF THE *KINGDOM OF GOD*. MATTHEW'S GOSPEL WAS DIRECTED TOWARD THE JEWS. JEWISH PIETY PROMPTED THEM TO AVOID USING THE WORD *GOD* AS A REMINDER OF THE SERIOUSNESS OF BLASPHEMY.

    We remember our Lord's teaching: *"It is easier for a camel to go through the eye of a needle than for someone who is rich to enter the kingdom of God." When the disciples heard this, they were greatly astounded, and said, "Then who can be saved?" But Jesus looked at them and said, "For mortals it is impossible, but for God all things are possible."*

MATTHEW 19:24-26

    If, with the disciples in this straightforward division between the rich and the poor, we see ourselves as rich simply because we are not poor, then God's miraculous power is needed to open the kingdom for us. When the poor hear the words, *yours is the kingdom of God*, they also know that only God's power could make this good news possible for them. The contradiction between these two versions of the first beatitude is more apparent than real.

THE TERM *MIDDLE CLASS* CAME INTO USE IN ENGLAND IN THE EARLY 1800'S. THE INDUSTRIAL REVOLUTION BEGAN ABOUT 1790.
WORLD BOOK ENCYCLOPEDIA,
2001 EDITION.

[20]

Yet, these two versions seem to suggest that our Lord's teaching creates a division between the poor and the rich. The poor are honored for their humility and the rich are put down because of their pride. To deal with this issue, we need to remind ourselves of a couple of basic principles of biblical interpretation.

First, we interpret the Bible as the historical record of God's unfolding plan of salvation. The covenant God made with Abraham in ancient times is seen with reference to the new covenant proclaimed by Jesus, the promised Messiah.

In the Old Testament, wealth was seen as evidence of God's blessing. Abraham and the men of faith who followed after him were rich. In the New Testament, Jesus does not turn his back on the rich but he does turn his face with compassion toward the poor. For both the rich and the poor, this is good news.

Second, we interpret biblical passages with reference to the historical period in which they were written. The beatitudes were written during the first century. What was it like to live in that century? We are now at the beginning of the twenty-first century. How are we to apply the teachings of Jesus for our lives in the years ahead?

To gain some perspective of life in the first century, we begin in the year 69 B.C. The Jewish queen-mother, Salome Alexandra, died; her sons vied for the throne. Civil war resulted. From Rome, Pompey sent a peace mission to Jerusalem. When it failed, he himself came to the Holy City, stopped the fighting by force, and annexed Palestine to the province of Syria.

The family of Herod, *one of the most devious political families in antiquity,* managed to retain the favor of those in power in Rome. Herod the Great was named King of Judea by Augustus Caesar in 40 B.C. After his death, Caesar divided the territories among Herod's three sons.

Christianity began within Judaism. Jesus was born a couple of years before the demise of Herod the Great in 4 B.C. Jesus died during the period when Pontius Pilate was the Roman governor of Judea (26-36 A.D.) Life in Palestine was one of restive Jewish submission to Roman domination. The Jews regarded foreign domination as unnatural and eventually intolerable.

RELATED NOTES AND OBSERVATIONS

GENESIS 17:1-2

LUKE 1:68-69;
HEBREWS 8:1-13

GENESIS 13:2

PSALM 112

MEANWHILE, IN ROME, JULIUS CAESAR WAS ASSASSINATED, MARC ANTHONY WAS HAVING AN AFFAIR WITH CLEOPATRA, AND AUGUSTUS CAESAR WAS COMING INTO POWER.
A SKETCH OF THE HISTORY AND GEOGRAPHY OF THE LANDS OF THE BIBLE, P. 33

LATER, JUDEA WAS TURNED OVER TO PONTIUS PILATE.

In 66 A.D., they revolted. The rebellion was suppressed in 70 A.D. In the process, the temple was destroyed. For Judaism, the destructioin of the Temple meant that the synagogue became the sole center for Jewish culture. Before the end of the century, the normative list of the sacred books in the Hebrew Bible, (our Old Testament) was developed.

The period following 70 A.D. was also a critical time for Christianity. The tension between synagogue and church increased as Christians continued to reach out to the Hellenistic Jews and to the Gentiles. There was a fresh outbreak of Christian literary activity *including the writing of the Gospels of Matthew, Mark, Luke and John.* The letters of St. Paul, originally written around 50 A.D., were also collected, copied, and circulated. The New Testament in Greek began to emerge. Christianity and Judaism also had available the Old Testament in Greek.

From the perspective of money during this first century, wealth was a reward for gaining favor with Rome. The Herodians gained wealth, the tax collectors gained wealth; both were despised by the people. At the other end of the economic spectrum were the slaves. Slavery was an accepted reality within Palestine and throughout the Roman Empire.

The Romans favored the Sadduccees who were given control over the Temple. The Pharisees *who occasionally accused one another of hypocrisy* were more patriotic and consequently more popular among the people. The Essenes were a highly disciplined religious group who cut themselves off from mainstream Judaism. The Zealots were known for their zeal in opposition to the Roman oppressors.

To gain a perspective for the 21st century, we begin with the 69th year of the 19th century. In 1869, Ulyesses S. Grant was inaugurated as President of the U.S. Economically, our country was experiencing a depression. Congress was proposing the 15th Amendment to the Constitution which gave voting rights to the former slaves. The Civil War, concluded on April 12, 1865, was a defining moment in the history of our country.

From the perspective of money, in 1869 the South was an economic disaster. The North, by comparison, was prospering in spite of the current depression. The South discovered that cotton was no longer king. The North was entering the Industrial Age.

RELATED NOTES AND OBSERVATIONS

MEANWHILE, DURING THE REIGN OF NERO, ROME BURNED. NERO NEEDED A SCAPEGOAT, AND CHOSE THE CHRISTIANS, OF WHOM MANY WERE JEWISH CONVERTS.

PERHAPS DURING THIS SAME ERA, IN ROME, ST. PETER AND ST. PAUL BECAME MARTYRS FOR THE FAITH.
A SKETCH OF THE HISTORY AND GEOGRAPHY IN THE LANDS OF THE BIBLE. P. 34

THE *SEPTUAGINT* VERSION BEGAN IN 250 BC WITH THE TRANSLATION OF THE FIRST FIVE BOOKS OF THE HEBREW BIBLE.

WANDERINGS,
BY CHAIM POTOK,
P. 280

PRESIDENT LINCOLN WAS ASSASSINATED TWO DAYS LATER.

THE INDUSTRIAL REVOLUTION WOULD MAKE THE TERM *MIDDLE CLASS* A DISTINCTIVE NECESSITY IN OUR COUNTRY.

The Industrial Age established a partnership between democracy and capitalism which *over the past 150 years was sustained by belief in an impersonal momentum of progress.* This progress was reflected in economic growth enough *to double real living standards every forty-seven years.* This doubling was achieved in spite of the depression in 1869 and the greater depression in the 1930's.

Looking back over the 20th century, with Jacob Needleman we may wonder: *How is it that after decades of inventions and new technologies devoted to saving time and labor, the result is that we have no time left? We are a time-poor society; we are temporally impoverished.*

With Lewis Lapham, we also ponder the conumdrum which was noted earlier: *Never in the history of the world have so many people been so rich; never in the history of the world have so many of those same people felt themselves so poor. It is an odd paradox . . .*

From our own experience, we may see ourselves as rich even when our economic status does not suggest wealth. We may remember years of financial scarcity when we did not feel poor. If we are now at a time when money is more than adequate for our needs, we are also aware that the possibility of poverty is never far removed from us. What does it mean to be rich? What does it mean to be poor?

In this first chapter on our Lord's teachings concerning money, we have scarcely scratched the surface. We have been reminded that complexity and simplicity go hand in hand. We may be confident that new dimensions pertaining to this first beatitude will be discovered as we pursue the teachings of our Lord.

RELATED NOTES AND OBSERVATIONS

ROBERT HEILBRONER,
21ST CENTURY CAPITALISM,
P. 150

21ST CENTURY CAPITALISM,
P. 56

JACOB NEEDLEMAN,
MONEY AND THE MEANING OF LIFE,
P. 29

LEWIS LAPHAM,
MONEY AND CLASS IN AMERICA,
P. 8

[C-5]   THE TEACHINGS OF JESUS —
              AT THE BEGINNING

RELATED
NOTES AND OBSERVATIONS

Personal Notes and Observations
   concerning financial and spiritual poverty.

*A few questions to prompt questions of your own
   related to your faith journey.*

In terms of your own faith journey, what does it mean to be poor? What does it mean to be rich?

How does your personal history help you to evaluate poverty and wealth?

Has doubling real living standards every 47 years had an effect on poverty in our country?

During your working life has your real living standard doubled?

IS USING THE
MIDDLE CLASS
CATEGORY A WAY
TO DENY OUR WEALTH
OR OUR POVERTY?

===

[C-5]   THE TEACHINGS OF JESUS —
              AT THE BEGINNING

Congregational Notes and Observations
   about financial and spiritual poverty.

*A few questions to prompt questions of your own
   related to your congregation's ministries.*

How does your congregation see itself as poor or as rich in monetary terms?

Was there a time when your congregation was monetarily poor? During that time was it spiritually rich?

Does it really make any difference how a congregation sees itself monetarily?

Does it take courage to celebrate the wealth of your congregation and the wealth of your members?

CONGREGATIONS CAN
USE THE *MIDDLE CLASS*
CATEGORY AS A WAY
TO AVOID DECLARING
THEMSELVES TO BE
WEALTHY OR POOR.

RECONCILIATION, THEN . . .

RELATED
NOTES AND OBSERVATIONS

So when you are offering your gift at the altar, if you remember that your brother or sister has something against you, leave your gift there before the altar and go; first be reconciled to your brother or sister, and then offer your gift.

MATTHEW 5:23-24

CONTEXT: MATTHEW 5:21-26

Reflecting on this teaching of Jesus brings to mind a passage from I John, a portion of one of the parables, and two stories from the New Testament, all of which give shape to this chapter.

The passage from the First Letter of John sharpens our focus: *Those who love God must love their brothers and sisters also.* The context of these words proclaims that *God is love;* and we *love because he first loved us;* and that those *who do not love a brother or sister whom they have seen, cannot love God whom they have not seen.*

I JOHN 4:21

I JOHN 4:16
I JOHN 4:19, 20

Reconciliation between members of the family of faith is of primary importance. It is one of our first goals as followers of Christ. Even our worship is to be interrupted in order to grasp an opportunity to make peace.

In the parable of The Prodigal Son, it is the elder brother who comes to mind. When he learned that his father had welcomed the prodigal son home, he was angry. He cried out to his father, *"Listen! For all these years I have been working like a slave for you . . .; yet you have never given me even a goat that I might celebrate with my friends."*

LUKE 15:29
CONTEXT: LUKE 15:25-32

If he had been at the house when his younger brother came with the confession, *"Father, I have sinned . . . I am no longer worthy to be called your son",* the coming celebration would not have been so offensive to the elder brother. For the sake of both brothers, immediate reconciliation was essential.

LUKE 15:21
CONTEXT: LUKE 15:11-24

In the first story from the New Testament, Ananias comes to mind. He was in Damascus as a follower of Christ when the Lord came to him in a vision. He was instructed to go immediately to minister to a man named Saul of Tarsus.

The reaction of Ananias reminds us of that elder brother in the parable. He can scarcely believe what he was asked to do. *"Lord, I have heard from many about this man, how much evil he has done to your saints . . ."* What Ananias had heard was true, but it was not the whole story.

He did not know what had happened to Saul on the road to Damascus. The Lord did not argue with Ananias. He said simply, *"Go, for he is an instrument whom I have chosen . . ."* Ananias became a minister of reconciliation as he brought the message, *"Brother Saul, the Lord Jesus . . . has sent me so that you may regain your sight and be filled with the Holy Spirit."*

Saul regained his sight and was baptized. For the rest of his life he would proclaim the message of the risen Christ to Gentiles and to Jews. Saul/Paul remains for us a teacher of the faith and an example of a godly life. Ananias was of critical importance during those days in Damascus. He is not mentioned again in the New Testament.

There are two parts to this teaching of Jesus which is the focus for this chapter. Leaving our gift at the altar in order to take care of first things first underscores our personal role in the ministry of reconciliation. The second part underscores the importance of offering our gifts to enable the church to continue its world-wide ministry of reconciliation.

It is this second part which brings to mind a second story from the New Testament. By this time, Paul was an *old man* and a *prisoner* persecuted for his faith in Christ. It is a story told in a very personal letter to a *dear friend* named Philemon who lived in Colossae. It is about *"Onesimus, whose father I have become during my imprisonment."*

This letter is only 25 verses long. It invites us to read between the lines as we meditate on the ministry of reconciliation in behalf of Onesimus. He was a slave who belonged to Philemon. Philemon had become a Christian through the ministry of Paul and Timothy. At the time this letter was written, Philemon was a leader within the church as other Christians gathered for worship at his house. At some point, Onesimus ran away from his master.

RELATED NOTES AND OBSERVATIONS

ACTS 9:13

ACTS 9:15

ACTS 9:17

ACTS 9:18

SEE ALSO ACTS 22:1-16

TWO DIFFERENT MEN WITH THIS SAME NAME ARE MENTIONED: SEE ACTS 5:1-5 AND ACTS 22:12.

PHILEMON 9

PHILEMON 1

PHILEMON 10
COLOSSIANS 4:9

We can use our imaginations to fill in the details. Arriving either in Rome or in Ephesus, Onesimus heard the news that Paul was in prison there. Perhaps he remembered when Paul became a friend of Philemon and how the life of his master was changed. Whatever the details may have been, Onesimus goes to Paul in prison; he remains close at hand and proves himself to be very helpful. At some point Onesimus confesses to Paul that he has run away from his master. As he comes to faith in Christ, it becomes of basic importance for Onesimus to be reconciled with Philemon.

The Letter to Philemon was both personal and pastoral. Paul wrote to him, not only as a dear friend but as a *co-worker.* This letter is about the church at work in the ministry of reconciliation. Paul encouraged Philemon to welcome Onesimus home, *no longer as a slave* but *as a beloved brother.*

We do not know what happened to Onesimus after Paul wrote this letter. One of the traditions from that era is that Philemon did set his slave free, and Onesimus, years later, became one of the bishops of the church. If that tradition is accurate, it would provide another reason for including this letter of Paul to Philemon in the New Testament.

Week after week, year after year, we offer gifts as acts of worship. We may wonder where our money travels, how it is put to work, and whose lives are transformed by the ministry of reconciliation. Then we shift our thinking and reflect on the faithful gifts of our ancestors. Their gifts which reached around the world over the past two millenia were put to work to transform our lives that we might be reconciled with God and with one another.

Now we must turn our attention to this new millenium. The enormous changes which have been part of our lifetimes are a prelude to the changes coming over the horizon. Its seems apparent that the basic need for reconciliation with God and with one another will continue, and, in addition, there will be an urgent need to be reconciled with the earth itself.

In this 21st century, achieving ecological goals will not be a matter of idealism but of survival. Just as every act in an industrial society leads to environmental degradation regardless of intention, a new system needs to be designed which is environmentally sustainable and restorative.

RELATED NOTES AND OBSERVATINS

PHILEMON 11

PHILEMON 16

THE NEW BIBLE DICTIONARY, P. 910-911.

PAUL HAWKIN, *THE ECOLOGY OF COMMERCE,* SUGGESTS AS OBJECTIVE #1: *REDUCE ABSOLUTE CONSUMPTION OF ENERGY AND NATURAL RESOURCES IN THE NORTH BY 80 PERCENT WITHIN THE NEXT HALF CENTURY.* HE INDICATES THAT WE ALREADY HAVE THE TECHNOLOGY TO DO THIS. P. XIV

In this 21st century, the religions of the world are emigrating to our country. Reconciliation between religions does not mean that Christians have forsaken the command to *Go . . . make disciples of all nations.* Reconciliation begins as we show love and respect for persons of other religions.

An illustration of this love and respect was a response to the book, *Abraham, A Journey to the Heart of Three Faiths.* It is a book which many Americans are reading. Some of these people go to churches, others to synagogues, and others to mosques. They have chosen to gather together as *Children of Abraham* to discuss what their faiths have in common.

Within this global neighborhood and the world market, preserving our planetary home as a place fit for human habitation will involve everyone working together everywhere.

RELATED NOTES AND OBSERVATIONS

MATTHEW 28:19

BY BRUCE FEILER

(C-6) RECONCILIATION, THEN . . .   RELATED NOTES AND OBSERVATIONS

Personal Notes and Observations
    related to reconciliation and its
    importance for your faith journey.

*A few questions to prompt questions of your own
related to your faith journey.*

Is there a need for you to be reconciled with someone you have chosen to neglect?

Do you have the courage to risk reconciliation with someone whom has chosen to neglect you?

Has this personal problem had a negative effect on your spiritual health, including your monetary stewardship?

CAN YOU REMEMBER A STEWARDSHIP PROGRAM WHICH GAVE RECONCILIATION THIS KIND OF PERSONAL PRIORITY?

Has the urgent need to be reconciled with the earth itself shaped your faith journey?

===

(C-6) RECONCILIATION, THEN . . .

Congregational Notes and Observations
    concerning reconciliation between members.

*A few questions to prompt question of your own
related to your congregation's ministries.*

How does the ministry of reconciliation shape the ministry of stewardship in your congregation?

PERHAPS THIS INSIGHT FROM *JESUS' TEACHINGS ABOUT MONEY* WILL PROVE TO BE ONE OF THE IMPORTANT STEWARDSHIP ISSUES TO BE CONSIDERED BY CONGREGATIONS.

As you reflect on the reasons why some members of your congregation are rarely at worship on an average Sunday, would reconciliation between members be a significant reason?

In your congregation how would you practice the ministry of reconciliation within the context of the Gospel?

A SPECIAL PLACE FOR THE POOR

RELATED NOTES AND OBSERVATIONS

When you give alms, do not let your left hand know what your right hand is doing.

MATTHEW 6:3
CONTEXT: MATTHEW 6:1-4

In the teachings of Jesus there is a special place for the poor. A special place is also created by this chapter. In the privacy of this place we can consider some of the thoughts that come to mind, including those we are not ready to discuss openly.

For instance, we may wonder why the poor merit a special place. Isn't the Bible very blunt in its teachings about the poor? Paul wrote, *Anyone unwilling to work should not eat.* Jesus said that the poor are a perennial problem, *For you always have the poor with you.* Why is an on-going problem given a special place? And why should gifts to the poor be offered with such secrecy? Jesus taught us, *Let your light shine before others so that they may see your good works and glorify your Father in heaven.*

2 THESSALONIANS 3:10

MARK 14:7 AND
MATTHEW 26:11

MATTHEW 5:16

Within the privacy of personal reflections we can take time to examine these passages in their context. We discover that the passage, *Anyone unwilling to work should not eat,* does not pertain to the poor at all. Members of the congregation in Thessalonica were convinced that the Second Coming of Christ was close at hand. For this reason, they decided to stop working. It is this issue that Paul raises in his letter to them, and about which he speaks so bluntly.

CONTEXT:
1 THESSALONIANS 5:1-11
AND
2 THESSALONIANS 3:1-13

Jesus taught us, *For you always have the poor with you.* The context of this verse is so rich, we will want to look at it more closely in a later chapter. For now, it is enough to note that Jesus does not view the poor as a perennial problem for us but as an on-going opportunity: *For you always have the poor with you, and you can show kindness to them whenever you wish.*

CONTEXT:
MARK 14:3-9 AND
MATTHEW 26:6-13

MARK 14:7

As we reflect on the various dimensions of poverty, we are grateful for this teaching of our Lord. When we are poor in health, we need tender loving care. When we are poor in spirit, we need the strong to help us through these troubles. When we are impoverished financially, a helping hand quietly given can give us hope and encouragement.

PSALM 103

ROMANS 14:1-23

Jesus taught us, *Let your light shine before others, so that they may see your good works and glorify your Father in heaven.* The point here is to let *your light* shine through *your good works* in order to *glorify your Father in heaven.* When we give to the poor, we are to do so privately lest we simply glorify ourselves.

As we reflect on a special place for the poor, it is easy to begin with negative thoughts. The harsh claim is made that a special place means that those who are not poor are put down. That deduction is not correct.

In writing to the Christians in Corinth about the poor in Jerusalem, Paul put it this way: *I do not mean that there should be relief for others and pressure on you, but it is a question of a fair balance between your present abundance and their need, so that their abundance may be for your need, in order that there may be a fair balance.*

This special place for the poor does not exclude the poor who want to be of help to other poor folks. Paul himself was astonished by the poor Christians in the churches of Macedonia who *during a severe ordeal of affliction, their abundant joy and their extreme poverty have overflowed in a wealth of generosity on their part. For as I can testify, they voluntarily gave according to their means, and even beyond their means, begging us earnestly for the privilege of sharing in this ministry to the saints.*

The special place for the poor is dramatically revealed on the Day of Judgment. *When the Son of Man comes in his glory . . . he will separate people one from another . . . Then the king will say to those on his right hand, 'Come, you who are blessed by my Father, inherit the kingdom prepared for you. . . for I was hungry . . . I was a stranger . . . I was naked . . . I was sick . . . I was in prison . . . Then the righteous will answer him, 'Lord, when did we see you hungry . . . or thirsty . . . or a stranger . . . or naked . . . or sick . . . or in prison . . .? And the king will answer them, ' . . . as you did it to one of the least of these who are members of my family, you did it to me.'*

RELATED NOTES AND OBSERVATIONS

MATTHEW 5:16

2 CORINTHIANS 8:13-14

2 CORINTHIANS 8:2-4

THE POOR ARE ALSO GIVEN A SPECIAL PLACE IN THE OLD TESTAMENT. NOTE PROVERBS 14:31 AND EZEKIEL 34:1-31

MATTHEW 25:31-40

The special place for the poor was also dramatically demonstrated during the early years in the history of the Church. We are told that *no one claimed private ownership of any possessions, but everything they owned was held in common.* Consequently, *there was not a needy person among them.*

ACTS 4:32

ACTS 4:34

The story of Ananias and Sapphira indicates the difficulty of this communal life style, but the special place for the poor continued within the Church. James, a brother of our Lord and a prominent leader within the Church, warns congregations against showing partiality which favors the rich over the poor. He concludes his admonition with these words, *You do well if you really fulfill the royal law according to the scripture, 'You shall love your neighbor as yourself.'*

ACTS 5:1-11

JAMES 2:1-7

JAMES 2:8

In Paul's first letter to Timothy, he wrote, *As for those who in this present age are rich, command them not to be haughty, or to set their hopes on the uncertainty of riches, but rather on God who richly provides us with everything for our enjoyment. They are to do good, to be rich in good works, and ready to share, thus storing up for themselves the treasure of a good foundation for the future, so that they may take hold of the life that really is life.*

I TIMOTHY 6:17-19

It is important to understand these teachings against the background of poverty and wealth during the 1st century. It is equally important to apply these teachings during these transition years at the beginning of the 21st century. *In a transition period, the number of people in need always grows.*

PETER F. DRUCKER, *POST-CAPITALIST SOCIETY,* P. 168

We are painfully aware of the great masses of refugees all over the globe, victims of war and social upheaval, of racial, political and religious persecution. Peter Drucker adds, *Even in the most settled and stable societies people will be left behind in the shift to knowledge work.* It will be the better part of a generation before the skills of service workers can provide them with a reasonable standard of living.

POST-CAPITALIST SOCIETY, P. 168

The business world has a history of providing jobs for the poor but the need for unskilled workers is rapidly diminishing. What is needed, says Drucker, is a *third sector, in addition to the generally recognized ones, the 'private sector' of business and the 'public sector' of government. It needs an autonomous 'social sector.'*

POST-CAPITALIST SOCIETY, P. 171

RELATED NOTES AND OBSERVATIONS

The *'social sector'* is composed of independent non-profit agencies, including churches, which have a record of success in dealing with social problems. A basic reason for their success is their partnership with new volunteers. *The great bulk of the new volunteers are not retired people; they are husbands and wives in a professional two-earner family, people in their thirties and forties, well-educated, affluent, busy. They enjoy their jobs. But they feel the need to do something where 'we can make a difference'.*

From the perspective of money, the future presents the possibility of a 'win-win' situation for all three sectors of society. Effective programs which provide a special place for the poor reduces the number of dependent persons as it creates new tax paying citizens. These programs also provide a greater number of skillful employees and paying customers.

Of greatest importance, providing a special place for the poor also creates a special place for those who *'make a difference'* by their voluntary efforts. From the perspective of our faith, our Lord tells us, *as you did it to one of the least of these who are members of my family, you did it to me.*

RELATED NOTES AND OBSERVATIONS

IN CHAPTER #3 WE NOTED THAT *MAMMON IS THE GOD OF AMERICA'S CIVIL RELIGION.* IT IS ALSO NOTEWORTHY TO ACKNOWLEDGE THAT ANOTHER DEFINING CHARACTERISTIC OF OUR CIVIL RELIGION IS ITS EXTENSIVE AND GENEROUS VOLUNTEERISM.

POST-CAPITALIST SOCIETY, P. 176

MATTHEW 25:40

[C-7]   A SPECIAL PLACE FOR THE POOR   RELATED NOTES AND OBSERVATIONS

Personal Notes and Observations
        related to a special place for the poor.

*A few questions to prompt questions of your own
    related to your faith journey.*

If you agree that this 21st century is a transitional time when giving for the poor needs special emphasis, how are you responding to the needs of the poor?

If you agree that during this time, you may experience poverty through no fault of your own, what role should Christians play in responding to your needs?

Have you discovered that creative giving for the poor can be a deeply satisfying experience?

THE PASTOR'S *DISCRETIONARY FUND* MAY PROVIDE A PRIVATE CHANNEL THROUGH WHICH A MEMBER OF THE CONGREGATION CAN PRIVATELY GIVE HELP TO ANOTHER MEMBER EXPERIENCING POVERTY.

===

[C-7]   A SPECIAL PLACE FOR THE POOR

Congregational Notes and Observations
        related to a special place for the poor.

*A few questions to prompt questions of your own
    related to your faith journey.*

How has your congregation responded to the needs of the poor in new and creative ways?

At the same time, how has your congregation provided opportunities for poor persons to give for the sake of other persons who are poor?

Do you know poor persons who correctly see themselves as rich, even as there are rich persons who correctly see themselves as poor?

GENEROSITY IS ONE OF THE WAYS THAT POOR PERSONS CAN GAIN AN EXPERIENCE OF FREEDOM FROM THE PAINS OF POVERTY.

[C-8]

TREASURES: ON EARTH, IN HEAVEN

RELATED
NOTES AND OBSERVATIONS

Do not store up for yourselves treasures on earth, where moth and rust consume and where thieves break in and steal; but store up for yourselves treasures in heaven, where neither moth nor rust consumes and where thieves do not break in and steal. For where your treasure is, there will your heart be also.

MATTHEW 6:19-21

Within the privacy of our personal reflections, we may choose to begin with two blunt questions: Why can't we have both? Isn't it possible to enjoy those things which may bring us some comfort and pleasure now and, at the same time, to live by faith with the assurance of treasures in heaven? Outlining a response to those questions is the goal of this chapter.

A closer look at this teaching of our Lord suggests that these words spoken in Aramaic were a form of poetry, portraying a kind of proverb or an embryo parable. This type of teaching easily clings within memory and prompts contemplation.

THE INTERPRETER'S BIBLE,
VOLUME 7, PAGES 317-318

The word *moth,* for our Lord's listeners in the 1st Century, brought to mind the wealth that was treasured in terms of expensive rugs and elaborate garments. Wealth also included tools and other treasures subject to rusting. The word *rust* included within it the picture of *rotting.* Rotting in those days long before refrigeration was a constant menace threatening expensive foods and elaborate feasting which marked the style of the wealthy. Then, as now, thieves and vandals put worldly treasures at risk.

IN THIS 21ST CENTURY,
ANALOGOUS WORDS FOR
MOTH AND *RUST,* WOULD
INCLUDE: INFLATION,
DOWNSIZING, OBSOLETE,
AND DEPRECIATION.

Teaching through proverbs brought to mind the writings attributed to Solomon, their wise and wealthy king from ancient times. As he reviewed his earthly treasures which provided him with a measure of comfort and pleasure, he concluded, *Then I considered all that my hands had done and the toil I had spent in doing it, and again, all was vanity and a chasing after wind, and there was nothing new to be gained under the sun.*

THE POETIC/PROVERBIAL
STYLE CONVEYS WISDOM
WHICH CONTINUES TO BE
APPRECIATED BOTH
WITHIN JUDAISM AND
CHRISTIANITY.

ECCLESIASTES 2:11
CONTEXT:
ECCLESIASTES 2:1-11

As an embryo parable, our Lord's teaching brings to mind *The Parable of The Rich Fool.* This story was told in response to a question from the crowd: *Teacher, tell my brother to divide the family inheritance with me.* Jesus was not offended by this request. He chose it to affirm a great truth about money.

LUKE 12:13

[35]

Speaking to a large crowd, Jesus said, *Take care! Be on your guard against all kinds of greed; for one's life does not consist in the abundance of possessions.*

LUKE 12:15

The parable of the rich fool is about a wealthy farmer who was enjoying bumper crops year after year. Finally, he had no place to store his treasures and made this decision: *I will pull down my barns and build larger ones, and there I will store all my grain and my goods. And I will say to my soul, Soul, you have ample goods laid up for many years; relax, eat, drink and be merry. But God said to him, You fool! This very night your life is being demanded of you. And these things you have prepared, whose will they be?*

LUKE 12:16-20

LUKE 12:18-20

Jesus told many parables, some of which were difficult to understand. For this parable, Jesus immediately made clear the point of it. *So it is with those who store up treasures for themselves but are not rich toward God.*

THIS PARABLE IN LUKE, LIKE THE EMBRYO PARABLE IN MATTHEW, PRECEDES OUR LORD'S TEACHING ENTITLED, *DO NOT WORRY* — CHAPTERS #11 AND #12 —

LUKE 12:21

As we consider the treasures of this world, we know that all these things are subject to the ravages of time, and so are we. We also acknowledge the fact that we never really possess these things with any permanence for our own lives are limited by circumstances over which we have no control. To think otherwise is to be a fool.

When we ask concerning treasures on earth and heaven — Why can't we have both? — we need to remember that we have no lasting claim on either.

Concerning earthly treasures, Solomon, in his wisdom, was bluntly realistic: *Again I saw that under the sun the race is not to the swift, nor the battle to the strong, nor bread to the wise, nor riches to the intelligent, nor favor to the skillful; but time and chance happen to them all. For no one can anticipate the time of disaster. Like fish taken in a cruel net, and like birds caught in a snare, so mortals are snared at a time of calamity, when it suddenly falls on them.*

WHETHER SOLOMON WAS THE AUTHOR OR WAS BEING HONORED BY AN UNKNOWN AUTHOR REMAINS A TOPIC FOR SCHOLARLY DEBATE. ECCLESIASTES 1:1, 12

ECCLESIASTES 9:11-12

During his lifetime, the apostle Paul had ample reasons to affirm the harsh realities described in Ecclesiastes. However, in his letter to Philippi, he was able to say, *I have learned to be content with whatever I have. I know what it is to have little, and I know what it is to have plenty. In any and all circumstances, I have learned the secret of being well-fed and of going hungry, of having plenty and being in want.*

PHILIPPIANS 4:11-12

Contentment was constant through all the circumstances of his life. He did not feel guilty during good times when he was blessed with plenty, and contentment remained during his most difficult days. In fact, Paul was in prison when he wrote these words. This letter was a thank-you note to his friends in Philippi for their on-going generosity.

RELATED NOTES AND OBSERVATIONS

PHILIPPIANS 4:15-19

Paul was a person who lived by high moral standards, but this was not the basis for his contentment. He knew himself to be *the foremost of sinners.* Nor did his contentment flow from robust good health. *A thorn in the flesh* was a painful reality throughout his adult life. He was blessed with high intelligence and a good education. He saw himself as *a fool for Christ.*

I TIMOTHY 1:15

2 CORINTHIANS 12:7
CONTEXT:
2 CORINTHIANS 12:7-10
1 CORINTHIANS 4:10

His contentment did not depend on a highly satisfying ministry. To be sure, there were places like Philippi which were very encouraging for him. At the same time, there was blatant immorality at Corinth which almost broke his heart. He lost his patience with the foolish Galatians who were so quickly forsaking the Gospel.

I CORINTHIANS 5:1-2
GALATIANS 1:6-9
AMAZINGLY, THIS FIRST LETTER TO CORINTH INCLUDES PAUL'S LYRICAL CHAPTER ABOUT LOVE (CH. 13), AND THE GALATIAN LETTER IS CALLED *THE MAGNA CHARTA OF CHRISTIAN LIBERTY.*

His personal life was not always pleasant. The *disaster* and *calamity* described in Ecclesiastes, Paul experienced in good measure. *Five times I have received from the Jews the forty lashes minus one. Three times I was beaten with rods. Once I received stoning. Three times I was shipwrecked; for a night and a day I was adrift at sea; on frequent journeys, in danger from rivers, danger from bandits, danger from Gentiles, danger in the city, danger in the wilderness, danger at sea, danger from false brothers and sisters; in toil and hardship, through many a sleepless night, hungry and thirsty, often without food, cold and naked. And, besides other things, I am under daily anxiety for all the churches.*

2 CORINTHIANS 11:24-28

Paul's contentment was undergirded by riches beyond the power of money to match. He described his wealth in this way: *For you know the generous act of our Lord Jesus Christ, that though he was rich, yet for our sakes he became poor, so that by his poverty you might become rich.* This was Paul's greatest treasure; this was where his heart was also. Here is the basis for his contentment on earth and for treasurers in heaven.

2 CORINTHIANS 8:9

These riches are made possible for us by grace through faith alone without any merit in us. These gifts from God are given moment by moment: the gift of life itself; the gift of love which makes our lives worth living; and the gift of God's amazing grace which lifts our vision of life into his holy presence.

For where your treasure is, there will your heart be also. Living with contentment as persons who have *become rich,* we need not be conquered by poverty nor corrupted by wealth.

Paul was brought up as a person of privilege within a family that was not poor. The disciples did not leave lives of poverty when they began to follow Christ. Some of our Lord's followers were men of wealth, and some wealthy women gave money generously to undergird our Lord's ministry.

For all of them, their heart, their primary allegiance, was no longer given to earthly wealth. Poverty was a real possibility they were willing to accept for they had discovered a greater treasure which enriches this life and lasts far beyond our earthly existence.

RELATED NOTES AND OBSERVATIONS

MATTHEW 6:21

2 CORINTHIANS 8:9

HIS FAMILY WAS PROSPEROUS ENOUGH SO THAT PAUL COULD ENJOY ROMAN CITIZENSHIP AND RECIEVE A SUPERB EDUCATION.

MATTHEW 27:57, JOHN 19:39
LUKE 8:1-3, MARK 15:40-41

[C-8]　　TREASURES: ON EARTH, IN HEAVEN

RELATED NOTES AND OBSERVATIONS

Personal Notes and Observations
　　reflecting on earthly and heavenly treasures.

A few questions to prompt questions of your own related to your faith journey.

What do you do when, with Solomon, you find yourself *chasing after wind?*

ECCLESIASTES 2:11

As you reflect on your own faith journey, is contentment a goal for your living and your giving?

St. Paul lived with contentment through all the difficulties he experienced in the 1st century. How can contentment be achieved in this 21st century?

======================================

[C-8]　　TREASURES: ON EARTH, IN HEAVEN

Congregational Notes and Observations
　　related to earthly and heavenly treasures.

A few questions to prompt questions of your own related to your congregation's ministries.

In 2 Corinthians 8:9, St. Paul proclaims the Gospel in monetary terms. Is the Gospel, as expressed in this way, at the heart of your congregation's stewardship ministry?

FOR YOU KNOW THAT GENEROUS ACT OF OUR LORD JESUS CHRIST, THAT THOUGH HE WAS RICH, YET FOR OUR SAKE HE BECAME POOR, SO THAT BY HIS POVERTY YOU MIGHT BECOME RICH.
2 COR. 8:9

If 2 Corinthians 8:9 is to serve as a foundation for your stewardship ministry, would a basic emphasis be on contentment with thanksgiving?

Do you consider contentment with thanksgiving to be a motivator for generous giving?

PHILIPPIANS 4:11-12

[C-9]

THE LINCHPIN:
THE PEOPLE OF GOD

RELATED NOTES AND OBSERVATIONS

You cannot serve God and wealth.

MATTHEW 6:24

The dictionary provides two definitions for a *linchpin*. The first is *a pin inserted through the end of an axle-tree to keep the wheel on*. That picture is too simple for our purposes here. A *linchpin* is also defined as *something that holds the various elements of a complicated structure together*. It is this picture which may prove helpful as we consider this central teaching of our Lord about money.

WEBSTER'S COLLEGE DICTIONARY,
P. 787.

On this journey through the Gospels from the perspective of money, monetary wealth may be defined as a *linchpin* which holds the various elements of our current and complicated economic structure together. This linchpin binds together economic structures, both multinational and local entities. This linchpin also has a profound impact on the people of God as they create and maintain economic structures to carry out their Gospel ministries.

This teaching of our Lord begins with a simple axiom: *No one can serve two masters.* It goes on to provide the basic logic which supports this axiom: *for a slave will either hate the one and love the other, or he will be devoted to the one and despise the other.* Then our Lord gives expression to one of his basic precepts: *You cannot serve God and wealth.* This precept is so fundamental two consecutive chapters are provided for our reflection.

MATTHEW 6:24

1 — THE PEOPLE OF GOD
2 — THE WORLD OF COMMERCE

One way of illustrating the central character of this teaching is to go back to the Ten Commandments. There are differing ways of numbering these commandments, but how they begin and how they end is very clear.

This is how they begin: *I am the Lord your God . . . you shall have no other gods . . . You shall not make for yourself an idol . . . You shall not make wrongful use of the name of the Lord . . . Remember the Sabbath day to keep it holy.*

EXODUS 20:2-11

As the people of God, our most basic goal is to cleanse our lives of idolatry. Therefore, we do not create idols; we do not make wrongful use of the name of our Lord; and we remember to keep the Sabbath day holy.

This is how the commandments end: *You shall not covet . . . .* Sinful coveting is synonymous with greed which is synonymous with idolatry. The language of the New Testament about the seriousness of greed is very strong. *Be sure of this, that . . . no one who is greedy (that is, an idolator), has any inheritance in the Kingdom of Christ and of God.* The beginning and the ending of the commandments make it clear: *No one can serve two masters . . . You cannot serve God and wealth.*

EXODUS 20:17

ECONOMY, SEXUALITY, AND KNOWLEDGE ARE THE CHIEF FIELDS IN WHICH IDOLATRY TAKE PLACE.
M. DOUGLAS MEEKS,
GOD THE ECONOMIST, P. 21

EPHESIANS 5:5

To illustrate this basic teaching, Jesus told *The Parable of the Dishonest Manager.* In the first century, it was not uncommon for a wealthy family to select a slave as a steward. The steward, recognized for his ability, was given authority over the other slaves and was the manager of the family's property. These stewards, whether slaves or free men, were not always honest.

LUKE 16:1-13
COMPARE
MATTHEW 24: 45-51

In this parable the scoundrel was not a slave but an employee. He was guilty of squandering his employer's property. When the owner learned what was happening, he said to him, *What is this that I hear about you? Give me an accounting of your management, because you cannot be my manager any longer.*

LUKE 16:2

As we reflect on this portion of the parable, we may conclude that this employer was rich but not very wise. Giving this crook time to prepare an account of his own dishonesty simply revealed him to be a clever crook. Even his employer who was the victim of his cleverness felt compelled to commend him *because he acted shrewdly.*

LUKE 16:8

What he did was use his employer's wealth as a linchpin binding this dishonest manager to his master's debtors. He cancelled their debts after receiving payment for only a portion of it. He created for himself a community of thieves where he would always be welcome.

Our Lord invites us to learn from the shrewdness of this crook. It can be helpful to compare what he has to say in three excellent translations.

RELATED NOTES AND OBSERVATIONS

1. The New Revised Standard Version states: *And I tell you, make friends for yourselves by means of dishonest wealth so that when it is gone, they may welcome you into the eternal homes.*

2. The Jerusalem Bible translates this verse as follows: *And so I tell you: use money, tainted as it is, to win you friends, and thus make sure that when it fails you, they will welcome you into the tents of eternity.*

3. The New English Bible provides this translation: *So I say to you, use your worldly wealth to win friends for yourselves, so that when money is a thing of the past you may be received into an eternal home.*

Our Lord does not idolize wealth. He sees it as he see us; *dishonest, tainted, worldly.* Our Lord does not demonize wealth. Money is often used for good purposes. Wealth, like us, is transient. It can, however, become a linchpin with eternal potential.

Jesus invites us to reflect on this question, *If . . . you have not been faithful with dishonest wealth, who will entrust you with the true riches?* He then affirms this basic precept, *You cannot serve God and wealth.*

Religious people have not always used money for good purposes. For a small amount of money, Judas became a betrayer. Money became a linchpin between the religious authorities and this unhappy disciple to bring about the execution of the Son of God. When Judas repented and threw the money back at them, they refused to accept it for it was *blood money.* Finally, they decided to use it to buy *the potter's field as a place to bury foreigners.*

Following his resurrection, money was a linchpin binding together the authorities and the guards. The soldiers agreed for a *large sum of money* to spread the story that the *disciples came by night and stole him away while they were asleep.* The authorities agreed to keep the guards out of trouble if the governor heard their story about being asleep while on duty.

These incidents mark the beginning of a sad history during which the people of God have idolized wealth.

RELATED NOTES AND OBSERVATIONS

LUKE 16:9

LUKE 16:9

LUKE 16:9

LUKE 16:11

LUKE 16:13

MATTHEW 26:14-16

30 PIECES OF SILVER =
30 DENARII =
WAGES FOR 30 DAYS
OF WORK FOR
A COMMON LABORER.

MATTHEW 27:3-10

MATTHEW 28:11-15

For a number centuries long ago, the church was caught up in the pursuit of possessions and power. The vast wealth of the church made a mockery of the Christian Gospel.

Tetzel, the fund raiser for building St. Peter's cathedral in Rome, traveled far and wide to proclaim the heresy, *As soon as the coin in the coffer rings, The soul from purgatory springs.* Similarly, in our day, the greed of some TV evangelists has made it apparent that dishonest wealth has been their primary goal.

HERE I STAND, A LIFE OF MARTIN LUTHER, BY ROLAND BAINTON. P. 74

The point we must accept is that the people of God are not immune to the idolatry which is created by greed. With this sad truth acknowledged, we can go on to reflect on the rest of the story.

We have already noted that the church began as a commune in which everyone shared their wealth so *there was not a needy person among them.* Communal living was not an abiding characteristic of the early church but sharing money for the sake of the poor has remained over the centuries.

ACTS 4:34

Tertullian, an early historian, *catalogues a long list of groups that were cared for by the Christian believers. They supported and buried the poor, supplied the needs of boys and girls destitute of means, cared for the elderly that were confined to the house, provided for those who suffered shipwreck, and gave to those who had been banished to islands or mines for their fidelity to Christ's cause.*

FREEDOM OF SIMPLICITY, BY RICHARD J. FOSTER, P. 54

One of the great preachers in the early church, Bishop John Chrysostom, stated, *Every day the church here feeds 3,000 people. Besides this, the church helps provide food and clothes for prisoners, the hospitalized, pilgrims, cripples, churchmen and others.*

FREEDOM OF SIMPLICITY, P. 54

Monasteries in many places provided food and clothing for the poor. In more recent centuries, William Booth established the *Salvation Army* in order to minister to the poorest of the poor in the worst slums in London.

Robert Raikes established the Sunday School movement in an attempt to provide educational opportunities for impoverished children on the only day they did not have to work — Sunday.

These few examples simply open the door for further reflection as we bring to mind persons and programs within, around, and far beyond our congregations. Wealth, often a modest amount of money, becomes the linchpin which binds together the people of God and their ministries around the world. Under the guidance of the Spirit, mountains are moved, the Gospel is lived out, and lives are transformed.

RELATED NOTES AND OBSERVATIONS

TWO OF THE LARGEST CHARITIES IN OUR COUNTRY ARE *CATHOLIC CHARITIES USA*, AND *LUTHERAN SERVICES IN AMERICA* WHICH INCLUDES *LUTHERAN SOCIAL SERVICES*.

[C-9] THE LINCHPIN: THE PEOPLE OF GOD

Personal Notes and Observations
    on the positive and negative sides of wealth.

A few questions to prompt questions of your own related to your faith journey.

During your faith journey, how have you dealt with the axiom, *You cannot serve God and wealth?*

MATTHEW 6:24

During your faith journey, how have you dealt with the problem of greed?

Within your family, how have you dealt with the problem of greed in discussions with your children?

[C-9] THE LINCHPIN: THE PEOPLE OF GOD

Congregational Notes and Observations
    concerning money as a linchpin.

A few questions to prompt questions of your own related to your congregation's ministries.

During the history of your congregation, have you experienced wealth as a linchpin to accomplish something memorable, perhaps miraculous?

Within your congregation has generosity been demonstrated more often among the rich than among the poor?

How does your congregation protect yourself from greed?

[C-10]

THE LINCHPIN:
THE WORLD OF COMMERCE

RELATED NOTES AND OBSERVATIONS

You cannot serve God and wealth.

MATTHEW 6:24
CONTEXT: MATTHEW 6:25-34
SEE ALSO: LUKE 12:22-34

Monetary wealth as a linchpin is not limited to the variety of ways in which the people of God facilitate their many ministries throughout the world. Wealth is also a linchpin for the commercial enterprises which surround us in our communities and include us in a world market. This basic precept in the teachings of our Lord, *You cannot serve God and wealth,* applies also to our lives in the world of commerce.

In the first century, it was easy to conclude that persons of wealth were greedy. In an earlier chapter, we noted that wealth was a reward for gaining favor with Rome. The Roman Empire was the enemy. Hence, the wealthy, many of whom were in league with the enemy, were despised by the people.

CHAPTER 5

Over the centuries, equating wealth with greed has remained commonplace. Christians have been quick to pity the poor and to blame the rich. We have not been as quick to remember that the disciples of our Lord did not leave poverty when they began to follow Christ, and that some of his followers were men and women of wealth.

In the first chapter on this basic precept, we reflected on *The Parable of the Dishonest Steward.* The biblical commentary on this parable concludes with the words, *You cannot serve God and wealth.* There is another parable, *The Parable of the Talents,* which merits our attention for two reasons.

LUKE 16:1-13

MATTHEW 25:14-30

First, it reminds us of the seriousness of greed. Greed, which is a form of idolatry, can put our eternal welfare in jeopardy. This parable appears immediately prior to *The Judgment of the Nations.* Secondly, the language of this parable reflects the language of the world of commerce.

MATTHEW 25:31-46

To this parable we owe another meaning to the familiar word, *talent*. The first meaning of this word refers to *a special, often creative natural ability or aptitude*. This parable has frequently been interpreted with this definition in mind so that a person with only one talent was seen as a rather common person.

In our Lord's day, a *talent* was a very old word referring to a large amount of money. In our dictionary this is now the 4th of 5 meanings to this word. In the footnote to this parable, this definition is given: *A talent was worth more than fifteen years' wages of a laborer.* As we interpret this parable from the perspective of money, it is this meaning that we have in mind.

This is the third in a series of parables leading up to *The Judgment of the Nations*. The purpose of these parables is to alert us to be prepared and to remain faithful. This parable is about a very rich man going on a journey who entrusted a considerable portion of his money to his slaves, *to one he gave five talents, to another two, and to another one, to each according to their ability.* Each of these slaves immediately became wealthy.

If a laborer in our time who has been averaging $30,000 a year was suddenly entrusted with $450,000, that person would be seen as wealthy. The fact that another person was entrusted with double that amount, and another five times that amount would not make the person with one talent common.

In this parable, *the one who had received five talents went off and traded with them, and made five more talents. In the same way, the one who had two talents made two more talents. But the one who had received one talent went off and dug a hole in the ground and hid his master's money. After a long time, the master of those slaves came and settled accounts with them.*

The point of the parable is that money is to be used creatively, making it possible for wealth to grow. Wealth is not to be buried, or hoarded. Using wealth creatively involves placing it at risk. This parable also points out that among us are persons who have greater ability than others for managing large amounts of money.

RELATED NOTES AND OBSERVATIONS

WEBSTER'S COLLEGE DICTIONARY,

INCIDENTALLY, MANY WORDS IN THE ENGLISH LANGUAGE HAVE MULTIPLY MEANINGS. FOR INSTANCE, THE WORD *CASE* HAS 29 DIFFERENT MEANINGS.

NEW REVISED STANDARD VERSION.

IN THE *NEW ENGLISH BIBLE,* A TALENT IS EQUATED WITH A BAG OF GOLD.

THE PARABLE OF THE CONSCIENTIOUS STEWARD, MATTHEW 24:45-51, *THE PARABLE OF THE TEN BRIDESMAIDS,* MATTHEW 25:1-13. (TITLES FROM *THE JERUSALEM BIBLE)*

THE NEW ENGLISH BIBLE TRANSLATES THE PHRASE *TRADED WITH THEM* AS *EMPLOYED THEM IN BUSINESS.*

A SOMEWHAT SIMILAR PARABLE IS *THE PARABLE OF THE POUNDS.* LUKE 19:11-27.

MATTHEW 25:16-19.

In the first chapter pertaining to wealth as *the linchpin*, we noted the sad history among the people of God when money was used for evil purposes. Over the centuries, the world of commerce has had its own sad history when greed has turned this *linchpin* into an idol.

Feudal lords in the Middle Ages, entrusted with the wealth of huge land holdings, kept the peasants who farmed the land perennially poor. Capitalists during the advent of The Industrial Age increased their wealth at the expense of the poor who lived in filthy slums. Conflicts, often violent, between labor and management were commonplace. In the pursuit of wealth, the environment has been victimized to the detriment of everyone, including future generations.

CHARLES DICKENS' PORTRAYAL OF EBENEZER SCROOGE IN THE UNABRIDGED VERSION OF *THE CHRISTMAS CAROL*, PUBLISHED IN LONDON, 1843, PROVIDES SHARP INSIGHTS INTO THIS ERA.

The point must be accepted that no one, regardless of class or station in life, is immune from the idolatry which is created by greed. With this sad truth in mind, we can go on to reflect on the rest of the story.

We no longer live in a time when wealth, class, and privilege are easily passed on from generation to generation. Nor do we live in a time when poverty is automatically perennial and unavoidable. Fortunately, the time has also passed when capitalists could routinely manipulate almost everything and everyone with the power of their wealth.

ROBERT HEILBRONER, IN HIS BOOK, *21ST CENTURY CAPITALISM*, PORTRAYS THE FUTURE DIFFERENTLY. THE TWENTY-FIRST CENTURY WILL BE DOMINATED BY A SPECTRUM OF CAPITALISMS, SOME SUCCESSFUL, SOME NOT.

THE CRUCIAL QUESTION FOR AMERICANS, AND PERHAPS FOR THE WORLD AS A WHOLE, IS WHERE OUR NATION WILL BE LOCATED ALONG THAT SPECTRUM P. 162-3

Indeed, Peter Drucker describes our time as a *Post-Capitalist Society. Instead of the old-time capitalist, in developed countries pension funds increasingly control the supply and allocation of money. In the United States, these funds in 1992 owned half of the share of capital of the countries largest businesses and held almost as much of these companies' fixed debts.* He goes on to say, *But equally important: the real resource and the absolutely decisive "factor of production" is now neither capital nor land nor labor: It is knowledge. Instead of capitalists and proletarians, the classes of the post-capitalist society are knowledge workers and service workers.*

POST-CAPITALIST SOCIETY, P. 6.

Yet, at the personal level, the emerging era means that we may see ourselves as capitalists. If we are contributing toward a pension fund, our wealth provides a key linchpin for commercial enterprises around the world.

If we are now living off our pension fund, the total amount we have contributed toward that fund plus accumulated earnings may equal one or more *talents* in the original meaning of that word.

This may mean we are free to set the boundaries as to how our wealth is to be put at risk. If the only guideline we promote is to achieve the greatest return possible, we may be guilty of greed. If we limit our investments to our own country, we may miss opportunities for ministry among the poor in other lands.

We also live in a time when business men and women who have been given talents for managing wealth may view these skills as gifts from God, and see their vocation in business as a calling from God. It is noteworthy that among the most prominent business leaders in our country, 35% of them worship each week and most of them are members of religious communities.

In recent years, business leaders have given expression to their religious convictions in what are called *The Minnesota Principles, Toward an Ethical Basis for Global Business*. These principles are now being studied nationally and internationally within the business community. The *General Principles* are these —

1. *Stimulating economic growth is the particular contribution of business to the larger society.*
2. *Business activities must be characterized by fairness.*
3. *Business activities must be characterized by honesty.*
4. *Business activities must be characterized by respect for human dignity.*
5. *Business activities must be characterized by respect for the environment.*

These *General Principles* are followed by *Stakeholder Principles*. According to these principles, attention is given first to *Customers,* then to *Employees,* then to *Owners/Investors*. The owners/investors who provide the wealth, the linchpin which holds the business together, are not given primary consideration. These principles indicate that the best, long-term way of honoring the trust that investors have placed in this business is to give higher priority to customers and employees.

RELATED NOTES AND OBSERVATIONS

CHURCH ATTENDANCE BY PROMINENT LEADERS IN THESE GROUPS:

	EVERY WEEK	NEVER
RELIGIOUS PROFESSIONALS	92%	0%
MILITARY OFFICERS	46%	13%
BUSINESS LEADERS	35%	13%
LABOR UNION LEADERS	31%	11%
BUREAUCRATS	25%	30%
FEDERAL JUDGES	17%	12%
CORPORATE LAWYERS	15%	24%
NEWS MEDIA	9%	48%
MOVIES	4%	63%

BUSINESS AS A CALLING, P. 43-45

FROM PAMPHLET PUBLISHED BY *MINNESOTA CENTER FOR CORPORATE RESPONSIBILITY,* COPYRIGHT, 1992.

These examples simply open the door for further reflection as we bring to mind persons and programs in the world of commerce where wealth is being used creatively for the greater good.

We are also reminded to pray for these key persons who have been given the talent to manage the many *talents* entrusted to them. For them, as for each of us, the temptation to practice greed can be as subtle as it is strong.

RELATED
NOTES AND OBSERVATIONS

(C-10)   THE LINCHPIN:
               THE WORLD OF COMMERCE

RELATED
NOTES AND OBSERVATIONS

Personal Notes and Observations
    reflecting on the world of commerce in your life.

A few questions to prompt questions of your own related to your faith journey.

If you are a salaried church worker, how much do you really know about how money works within the world of commerce?

If you earn your money within the world of commerce, how much do you really know about how money works within the church?

Do you agree that now knowledge is more powerful than money within the world of commerce?

IN MANY CONGREGATIONS, THE BIGGEST BLOCK OF MEMBERS ARE INVOLVED, IN VARIOUS WAYS, WITHIN THE WORLD OF COMMERCE.

===

(C-10)   THE LINCHPIN:
               THE WORLD OF COMMERCE

Congregational Notes and Observations
    related to the church and the world of commerce.

A few questions to prompt questions of your own related to your congregation's ministries.

Is it true that local business leaders may see local congregations as customers who often expect special consideration?

Is it often true that congregational leaders may not appreciate the difficulties faced by business leaders in a world-wide competitive environment?

Is it possible that money as a linchpin can serve to bring together congregational leaders and business leaders within their community?

[C-11]

ECONOMICS AND THE KINGDOM: A PERSONAL EVALUATION

RELATED NOTES AND OBSERVATIONS

*Do not worry about tomorrow,
for tomorrow will bring worries of its own.*

MATTHEW 6:34

CONTEXT: MATTHEW 6:25-34
SEE ALSO: LUKE 12:22-34

From the perspective of money, the economics related to this teaching of our Lord merit both a personal evaluation and then some reflections within the broad scope of history.

At the personal level, we note that the Matthew account of this teaching is preceded by *You cannot serve God and wealth,* and followed by *Do not judge, so that you may not be judged.* The parallel account in Luke presents this teaching as preceded by *The Parable of the Rich Fool,* and then followed by *For where your treasure is, there will your heart be also.*

MATTHEW 6:24

MATTHEW 7:1

LUKE 12:13-21

LUKE 12:34

To *worry about tomorrow* may be inevitable as we confront an unknown future. It is easy to be worried when we have left behind the familiar sights and sounds and routines which have moved into the past so quickly.

In the 1930's our nation was engulfed in the Great Depression. Widespread hunger and homelessness brought misery to people all around us. In 1933 our new president, Franklin D. Roosevelt proclaimed.
The only thing we have to fear is fear itself.
At that moment, it was difficult to take him seriously. Looking back, we recognize his prophetic correctness.

MY FELLOW AMERICANS,
MICHAEL WALDMAN,
P. 98

In 1939, the English poet, W. H. Auden, went into a nightclub on 52nd Street in New York City. Seated alone at a table, he studied the faces of men and women gathered there. Turning over the menu, he wrote these words:

52

Faces along the bar
Cling to their average day;
The lights must never go out,
The music must always play, . . .
Lest we should see who we are,
Lost in a haunted wood,
Children afraid of the night
Who have never been happy or good.

RELATED NOTES AND OBSERVATIONS

THE COLLECTED POETRY OF W. H. AUDEN, P. 38

At this point in our history, we were just emerging from the Great Depression. War was raging in Europe. Hitler was conquering one country after another. Our allies were pleading for help. We were afraid lest economic misery be followed by wartime horror.

AFTER PEARL HARBOR WE FOUGHT AND WON WW2 WITH OUR MILITARY MIGHT. WE WON THE PEACE WITH THE MARSHALL PLAN.

Anxiety blinds us to our worth as children of God and to the worth of our neighbors on this small planet. Anxiety is antithetical both to abundant living and to faithful discipleship.

Anxiety is alert to every evidence which can justify its continued existence in our lives. When Jesus told his disciples, *Do not worry about your life, what you shall eat or what you shall drink, or about your body, what you shall wear,* we bring to mind people who are hungry and thirsty and shabbily dressed.

MATTHEW 6:25

When our Lord poses the question, *And can any of you by worrying add a single hour to your span of life?*, he uses a bit of humor to combat the anxiety which prompts us to worry about what would happen to our family if we died prematurely.

MATTHEW 6:27
THE KING JAMES VERSION PROVIDES A LITERAL TRANSLATION OF THIS VERSE: *WHICH OF YOU BY TAKING THOUGHT CAN ADD ONE CUBIT UNTO HIS STATURE?* THE HUMOR IS APPARENT WHEN WE REMEMBER THAT A *CUBIT* IS ABOUT 18 INCHES LONG. FEW ADULTS WORRY ABOUT OR WOULD WANT TO BE 18 INCHES TALLER.

When Jesus teaches by examples from nature, saying, *Look at the birds of the air . . . Consider the lilies of the field . . .* the worrier brings to mind the forces of nature as it nurtures and then, too often, destroys the beauties of the earth.

MATTHEW 6:26-28

The 20th Century was known as *The Age of Anxiety.* Economic ups and downs, a cold war spawning war after war which could not be won, prompted many Americans to see themselves as —

Lost in a haunted wood,
Children afraid of the night,
Who have never been happy or good.

As we move into the 21st century, this teaching of Jesus is as pertinent for us as it was in the 1st century. His words convey compassion underscored with a bit of humor. Arguing with a worrier is a waste of time. In Matthew's account, he concludes by saying, *So do not worry about tomorrow, for tomorrow will bring worries of its own. Today's trouble is enough for today.* In Luke's account, he says, *Do not be afraid, little flock, for it is your Father's good pleasure to give you the kingdom.*

MATTHEW 6:27
MATTHEW 6:34
LUKE 12:32

As we listen from the perspective of money, we are confronted with some basic economic fears. These fears relate to our need for food and clothing, and our own mortality. Jesus encourages us to measure our fears by the economy of the Kingdom. *Life is more than food, and the body more than clothing. . . . How much more value are you than the birds! . . . If God so clothes the grass of the field . . . how much more will he clothe you — . . . Strive for his kingdom, and all these things will be given to you as well.*

LUKE 12:23
LUKE 12:24
LUKE 12:28
LUKE 12:31

The Kingdom of God bridges two worlds. We live within this Kingdom now as a gift of God's grace. This Kingdom will engulf us to the fullest in the world to come. The Kingdom of God bridges the reality of abundant living now and eternal life in his presence. He taught us to pray, *Your kingdom come. Your will be done on earth, as it is in heaven.*

MATTHEW 6:10

The economics of this world is based on scarcity. Scarcity of food and clothing means that the poor will be hungry and in rags. The economics of the Kingdom is based on abundance: *all these things will be given to you as well.* Trusting the truth of this teaching can be a liberating experience.

MATTHEW 6:33

How easily our worries shift from needs to wants. We are not anxious about going hungry, but about our hunger for special foods together with our worries about obesity. We are not worried about shabby clothing but about having suitable clothing for every occasion. Soon, luxuries become wants which become necessities.

IN DANTE'S *DIVINE COMEDY*, THE AUTHOR DESCENDS INTO HELL AND BEGINS TO FEEL SORRY FOR THE PEOPLE HE SEES THERE, WRITHING IN FILTH AND PAIN.

When worry is replaced with trust, our lives can move into a new direction. As we walk with the disciples during the ministry of Jesus, we are reminded again and again that their frail humanity is akin to our own. Then, in the wake of the resurrection, they were empowered by the Spirit to change the course of human history.

Do not be afraid, little flock, for it is your Father's good pleasure to give you the kingdom.

Within the kingdom now, our Father has given us the Word and the Sacraments, the promise that Jesus is present with us, and the guidance of the Holy Spirit. With these gifts, each day is to be celebrated with thanksgiving. With these gifts, each day brings opportunities to share with our neighbors near and far, by word and by deed that Christ has risen and we are victorious in his name.

RELATED NOTES AND OBSERVATIONS

BUT THE GREAT POET, VIRGIL, ADMONISHES HIM, *DO NOT FEEL PITY, THEY ARE GETTING EXACTLY WHAT THEY WANT. HELL IS THE STATE IN WHICH WE ARE BARRED FROM RECEIVING WHAT WE TRULY NEED BECAUSE OF THE VALUE WE GIVE TO WHAT WE MERELY WANT.*

MONEY AND THE MEANING OF LIFE, P. 27

LUKE 12:32

[C-11]   ECONOMICS AND THE KINGDOM:
        A PERSONAL EVALUATION

RELATED
NOTES AND OBSERVATIONS

Personal Notes and Observations
     reflecting on money and anxiety.

*A few questions to prompt questions of your own
related to your faith journey.*

As you consider your own money, how have you dealt with the problems which filled you with anxiety?

A SURPLUS OF MONEY AS WELL AS A SCARCITY OF MONEY PROVIDES A BASIS FOR ANXIETY.

Do you conquer your anxiety by contemplating on the fact that by faith you live in two kingdoms, one based on scarcity and the other based on abundance?

As you contemplate your anxieties are they more related to wants than to needs?

===

[C-11]   ECONOMICS AND THE KINGDOM:
        A PERSONAL EVALUATION

Congregational Notes and Observations
     related to money and anxiety in your congregation.

*A few questions to prompt questions of your own
related to your congregation's ministries.*

Do you think that anxiety is a basic cause for the lack of generosity to support the ministries of your congregation?

If this is true, how is your congregation comforting and then empowering these members?

Is this a dimension of your stewardship ministry which your committee and the evangelism committee will want to consider together?

A COMMON COMPLAINT AGAINST CONGREGATIONS IS, *THEY ARE ALWAYS TALKING ABOUT MONEY!*

ARE WE TO HEAR THESE COMPLAINTS AS AN INDICATION OF ANXIETY?

[C-12]

ECONOMICS AND THE KINGDOM: THE BROAD SCOPE OF HISTORY

\RELATED NOTES AND OBSERVATIONS

Strive first for the kingdom of God and his righteousness and all these things will be given to you as well.

MATTHEW 6:33

CONTEXT: MATTHEW 6:25-34
SEE ALSO: LUKE 12:22-34

In our first consideration of this text, we noted that the economics of this world is based on scarcity. The economics of the Kingdom of God is based on abundance. The relationships between the economics of this world and the economics of the Kingdom of God merit reflection within the broad scope of history.

As we think about the economics of this world, we begin with money. Milleniums ago, man invented money. The necessity which prompted the birth of this invention was to find something of value to trade for various commodities and as compensation for labor. With the passage of time, gold, silver, and copper became the primary metals from which money was made.

Relative scarcity gave value to these metals. However, money in terms of gold and silver had a serious drawback: it could be hoarded. Hoarding money took it out of circulation, thus creating problems in the world of commerce.

BEFORE THE CIVIL WAR IN OUR COUNTRY, PAPER MONEY WAS ISSUED BY STATE-CHARTERED PRIVATE BANKS. BANK FAILURES WERE COMMON; FINANCIAL PANIC FREQUENTLY FOLLOWED.

About half a millenium ago, the printing press was invented. Among the many uses for this new invention was the printing of money. Paper had little intrinsic value so this money was redeemable for gold. Maintaining adequate gold reserves to cover the paper money in circulation created new problems.

AFTER THE CIVIL WAR, PAPER MONEY WAS ISSUED ONLY BY NATIONAL BANKS.

AFTER THE FEDERAL RESERVE ACT IN 1912, PAPER MONEY WAS ISSUED ONLY BY THE 12 RESERVE BANKS. IN 1934, PAPER MONEY WAS NO LONGER REDEEMABLE IN GOLD. IN 1970, SILVER COINS WERE DISCONTINUED.

In this century, paper money is no longer redeemable for gold and our coins no longer contain precious metals. The trustworthiness of U.S. currency is not based on scarcity (gold and silver) but on the abundance of our national resources and the basic integrity of our democracy.

MONEY: ITS ORIGIN, DEVELOPMENT, AND MODERN USE, CARL H. MOORE, AND ALVIN E. RUSSELL.

Currently, our paper money and coins are being used primarily for incidental expenses. The great majority of our financial transactions are made with credit cards, checks, and Electronic Fund Transfers to and from our bank accounts.

During most of the milleniums of human history, agriculture has been the major focus of economic activity. The great majority of workers labored in the vineyards and out in the fields for the scarcity of food was a perennial problem. Crop failures meant famine.

In recent centuries, the increasing world population produced dire predictions of widespread starvation. It was believed that there were limitations as to the amount of food which could be produced on our planet. Scarcity appeared to be a harsh reality which could never be conquered.

Currently, less than 4% of our workers are engaged full-time in agriculture. Enough food is produced, not only for our nation; our farmers are looking for new markets in other countries. At the same time, the technologies which have transformed our agriculture are being exported to more primitive societies. Soon, these third world countries, where food had been an on-going scarcity, began to export their surplus. The problems related to scarcity are being changed into new problems associated with abundance.

During most of the milleniums of human history, economic advances were impeded by the scarcity of information. A crop failure in one region was particularly tragic if, a short distance away, there was food in abundance, some of it rotting in the fields. Equally unfortunate, if an abundant crop was the result of ingenuity or an accidental discovery as to how to grow more food, and that information could not be shared beyond their immediate community, then progress was severely limited and starvation remained a perennial possibility.

Currently, the ubiquitous computer has introduced The Information Age. Not only is information available in abundance, the computer is able to make it available almost everywhere at once.

RELATED NOTES AND OBSERVATIONS

THE *WORLD POLICY JOURNAL* STATES THE GLOBAL CURRENCY MARKETS *NOW TRADE OVER $1.1 TRILLION DOLLARS EACH DAY.*

85% OF THE WORLD'S POPULATION HAD TO WORK IN AGRICULTURE JUST TO PRODUCE ENOUGH FOOD.

FINANCIAL SUCCESS, GARY MOORE, P. 33

THE REVEREND THOMAS MALTHUS MORE THAN A CENTURY AGO, PREDICTED THAT MANKIND WAS DOOMED BECAUSE OUR GOD-GIVEN RESOURCES COULD NEVER FEED OUR GROWING POPULATIONS.

FINANCIAL SUCCESS, P. 155

THIS ALSO SUGGESTS THAT SMALLER RURAL CONGREGATIONS HAVE MEMBERS WITH THE TALENTS TO FARM LARGE ACREAGES. IN THIS 21ST CENTURY THESE RURAL CONGREGATIONS BECOME LARGER AS THEY FOCUS ON A WORLD-WIDE VISION, EVEN AS LARGE SUBURBAN CONGREGATIONS BECOME SMALLER AS THEY FOCUS ON MEETING THE NEEDS OF INDIVIDUAL MEMBERS.

In the emerging era, the principle resource for the production of goods and services to satisfy the marketplaces of the world is neither money nor land nor labor. It is knowledge. Obviously, land, as a metaphor for all the scarce physical resources with which we work, and money, as a linchpin which allows complex organizations to function effectively, remain essential but knowledge workers are becoming the determining factor for a successful enterprise. Knowledge workers are scarce but knowledge is not a non-renewable resource.

Knowledge is instrumental both in creating new wealth and new forms of scarcity. When super abundance becomes routine, then boring, there can be a deep desire for goods and services which are so specialized and scarce, monetary wealth is essential to satisfy this hunger.

As we begin to compare the economy of this world to the economy of the Kingdom, we see both similarities and differences. Jesus uses parables to describe the value of the Kingdom in terms of scarcity: *The Kingdom of heaven is like a merchant in search of fine pearls; on finding one pearl of great value, he went and sold all that he had and bought it.* There are also similarities in language. In both economies *one regularly hears such words as trust, fidelity, fiduciary, promissory, debt, saving, redemption, security, futures, bond, and so on.*

The differences begin to become apparent as we reflect on the root word for economy which is the Greek word *oikonomia*. This word is a compound of *oikos* = house, household; and *nomos* = law. *In classical Greek it had a variety of connotations but principally that of financial administration, the meaning retained in its direct derivatives such as economy and economics.*

In the New Testament, *oikonomia* is translated in various ways to express its shades of meaning. For instance, *oikonomos* is translated *manager,* a person who was entrusted with both the personnel and the possessions of the household. *Who then is the faithful and prudent manager whom the master will put in charge of the slaves, to give them their allowance of food at the proper time? . . . He will put that one in charge of his possessions.*

RELATED NOTES AND OBSERVATIONS

KNOWLEDGE WORKERS ARE NOW BEING RECRUITED WORLD-WIDE. UNSKILLED WORKERS ARE BECOMING AN ECONOMIC LIABILITY IN ADVANCED COUNTRIES.

MATTHEW 13:45-46

GOD THE ECONOMIST, M. DOUGLAS MEEKS, P. 29

A THEOLOGY FOR CHRISTIAN STEWARDSHIP, T. A. KANTONEN, P. 2

OTHER DERIVATIES OF THIS WORD ARE *ECUMENISM* AND *ECOLOGY.*

LUKE 12:42, 44

In the letters of Paul, *oikonomia* is translated as *steward* or *commission,* and becomes a major theological concept. Speaking of teachers who were called to serve the church, he writes, *Think of us in this way, as servants of Christ and stewards of God's mysteries.* Concerning himself as *a prisoner for Christ Jesus,* Paul writes about *the commission of God's grace that was given me for you, and how the mystery was made known to me by revelation . . .*

Oikonomia is used in its ultimate sense as it relates to the *plan* for the grand purpose of God. *With all wisdom and insight he has made known to us the mystery of his will, according to his good pleasure that he set forth in Christ, as a plan for the fulness of time, to gather all things in him in heaven and things on earth.*

The economics of the Kingdom begin with a focus on *oikos,* home, household. In this household, the people of God work and witness within the economics of this world governed by scarcity. Their faith gives them the freedom to work and witness within the economy of the Kingdom which is governed by abundance.

As Jesus introduces the central theme for his preaching ministry, he begins with this command and promise: *Strive first for the Kingdom of God and his righteousness, and all these things will be yours as well.*

RELATED NOTES AND OBSERVATIONS

I CORINTHIANS 4:1; SEE ALSO I PETER 4:10 AND MATTHEW 13:11

EPHESIANS 3:1-3
THE RSV TRANSLATES THIS PHRASE
THE STEWARDSHIP OF GOD'S GRACE THAT WAS GIVEN ME FOR YOU.

EPHESIANS 1:8-10

MATTHEW 6:33

[C-12]   ECONOMICS AND THE KINGDOM:
         THE BROAD SCOPE OF HISTORY

                                                                         RELATED
                                                                        NOTES AND OBSERVATIONS

Personal Notes and Observations
    related to the central theme of Jesus' teachings.

    A few questions to prompt questions of your own
                related to your faith journey.

    As you review your faith journey, do you see yourself as a steward of God's mysteries?

1 CORINTHIANS 4:1

    Do you view your monetary offerings as gifts empowered by the Gospel?

IT IS COMMONPLACE IN OUR COUNTRY FOR CHARITABLE CONTRIBUTIONS TO BE CONSIDERED AS INCIDENTAL EXPENSES.

    What illustrations come to mind which underscore what happens when gifts empowered by the Gospel are transformed into action?

    With these illustrations in mind, do you view the moments when the offering is received as a fundamental part of your worship experience?

FOR FOLLOWERS OF CHRIST, OUR GIFTS THROUGH OUR CHURCH ARE OF PRIMARY IMPORTANCE IN OUR FINANCIAL PLANNING.

==

[C-12]   ECONOMICS AND THE KINGDOM:
         THE BROAD SCOPE OF HISTORY

Congregational Notes and Observations
    related to the central them of Jesus' teachings.

    A few questions to prompt questions of your own
                related to your congregation's ministries.

    Does your congregation's annual financial report illustrate how the giving of members, empowered by the Gospel, has been transformed into action within, around, and far beyond your congregation?

    Can an annual financial report have this focus and, at the same time, assure members that good stewardship of income and expenses has been practiced?

THE TECHNOLOGY AVAILABLE TO MANY CONGREGATIONS MAKE IT POSSIBLE TO PRESENT FINANCIAL REPORTS IN WAYS THAT ARE INTERESTING, INFORMATIVE AND ATTRACTIVE.

[C-13]

MINISTRY WITHOUT MONEY

RELATED NOTES AND OBSERVATIONS

You received without payment; give without payment. Take no gold, or silver, or copper in your belts . . .

MATTHEW 10:8,9
CONTEXT: MATTHEW 10:1-15
SEE ALSO: MARK 6:7-13,
LUKE 9:1-6, 10:1-12

Mission statements are common among congregations and among commercial enterprises. What is uncommon, especially among congregational mission statements, is any reference to money.

In this chapter we are confronted with instructions which our Lord gave to his disciples when he sent them out on their first mission. This mission statement begins, *Go . . . to the lost sheep of the house of Israel . . . Proclaim the good news, 'The Kingdom of heaven has come near'. Cure the sick, raise the dead, cleanse the lepers, cast out demons.*

MATTHEW 10:5-9

The parallel passage in Luke abbreviates the first portion of this mission statement in Matthew. Luke states, *He (Jesus) called the twelve together and gave them power over all demons and to cure diseases, and he sent them out to proclaim the kingdom of God and to heal.* He continued with these specific directions, *Take nothing for your journey, no staff, nor bag, nor bread, nor money — not even an extra tunic.*

LUKE 9:1-2

LUKE 9:3
LUKE ALSO WRITES ABOUT
THE MISSION OF THE SEVENTY.
AGAIN, THE INSTRUCTIONS
ARE SPECIFIC:
CARRY NO PURSE, NO BAG, NO SANDALS.
LUKE 10:1-12

Mark, with typical brevity, tells us, *He (Jesus) called the twelve and began to send them out two by two, and gave them authority over unclean spirits.* Mark also includes these specific instructions: *He ordered them to take nothing for their journey except a staff; no bread, no bag, no money in their belts; . . .*

From the beginning of our journey through the Gospels, we noted that Jesus spoke about money always within the context of more important concerns. It is particularly apparent in this passage that money is surrounded by concerns of greater importance. For this reason, we shall begin with what is the most important in order to gain an appropriate understanding of the place of money within this mission statement.

Matthew was very specific as to where the disciples were to go on this first mission. *Go nowhere among the Gentiles, and enter no town of the Samaritans, but go rather to the lost sheep of the house of Israel.* We are not surprised that this first mission of the disciples was to *the lost sheep* of the house of Israel. *These may have been the* AMHAAREZ, *the "people of the land" or country people, careless of the details of the law, whom the Pharisees regarded with contempt.*

Throughout his ministry, Jesus frequently expressed his concern for those who were *lost,* especially among his own people. Congregational leaders may need to develop a specific mission strategy to win back members of their family of faith who have lost their way.

Jesus equipped his disciples for this mission. *Then Jesus summoned his twelve disciples and gave them authority over unclean spirits, to cast them out, and to cure every disease and every sickness.* Of first importance, he gave them this command: *As you go, proclaim the good news, 'The Kingdom of heaven has come near'.* The proclamation of the Gospel takes precedence over the ministry of healing. The Gospel provides healing for both body and soul. Its redemptive power embraces both time and eternity.

As the disciples went out, *two by two,* they were to be treated with respect. *Whatever town or village you enter, find out who in it is worthy, and stay there until you leave.* *Worthy* does not mean wealthy, but worthy to receive messengers of the Gospel. If the disciples were not welcomed, they were instructed to leave that place to the judgment of God.

Both Mark and Luke comment on what happened during this first mission endeavor. *So they went out and proclaimed that all should repent. They cast out many demons, and anointed with oil many who were sick and cured them. They departed and went out through the villages, bringing the good news and curing diseases everywhere.*

RELATED NOTES AND OBSERVATIONS

MATTHEW 10:5,6

THE GREAT COMMISSION IS A MUCH BROADER MISSION STATEMENT, INCLUDING GENTILES, SAMARITANS, AND EVERYONE ELSE ON OUR PLANET.
MATTHEW 28:19

THE INTERPRETER'S BIBLE, VOLUME 7, P. 365

SEE LUKE 15:1-7 AND MATTHEW 15:21-28

MATTHEW 10:1

MATTHEW 10:7

MARK 6:7

MATTHEW 10:11

MATTHEW 10:12-15

MARK 6:12, 13

LUKE 9:6
THE *MISSION OF THE SEVENTY* EXPERIENCED SIMILAR RESULTS.
SEE LUKE 10:17-20

The command — *You received without payment, give without payment* — remains a prime directive for the people of God. The *good news* which we received by grace alone and which has transformed our lives is not to be offered to others as a commercial commodity.

The command — *Take no gold, or silver, or copper in your belts* — which, in Mark and Luke is stated simply — *take . . . no money* — is emphasized in this mission statement but is absent from THE GREAT COMMISSION. The emphasis here is indicated by overstatement in Matthew and understatement in Mark and Luke.

In ancient times, gold was the currency of kings who used it in interstate transactions. It is highly unlikely that the disciple band had any gold in their treasury. In Mark the word *money* is the translation given for the word *silver*. *Copper* referred to pennies, the smallest, least valuable coins in Palestine.

In addition, the command in Matthew continues *take . . . no bag for your journey, or two tunics, or sandals, or a staff. . . .* Mark and Luke have similar lists. Further emphasis is given to these commands toward the close of our Lord's ministry. Jesus said to his disciples, *When I sent you out without purse, bag, or sandals, did you lack anything?* Without hesitation, the disciples replied, *No, not a thing.*

It is apparent that this was an important command. It is also apparent that these instructions were not given to make the lives of the disciples more difficult as they went on their first mission. What, then, was its purpose? As we noted, this command is not a part of THE GREAT COMMISSION. Does this mean that this command pertains only to that first mission for the disciples, or are there times when it remains an important command for us in our day?

These chapters provide a basis for further reflection. These reflections are drawn out of our own understanding of the teachings of Jesus, our own life experiences, and where we are at on our own faith journey. Candid conversation among friends will give voice to other reflections which will differ from or add new insights to those which follow here.

RELATED
NOTES AND OBSERVATIONS
MATTHEW 10:8

JOHN 3:16,17

MATTHEW 10:9

MARK 6:7; LUKE 9:3
MATTHEW 28:19

IN CONTEMPORARY
LANGUAGE, THESE
INSTRUCTIONS COULD BE
TRANSLATED AS
*TAKE NO CREDIT CARDS,
NOR CASH; NOT EVEN YOUR
PENNIES.*

MATTHEW 10:10

LUKE 22:35

MATTHEW 28:19

As we review this mission statement, we remember that its focus was on members of the family of faith who were *lost*. Perhaps we would use the word LAPSED. Or, perhaps we would view them as FREE SPIRITS, going their own way in the search for new meanings for their lives. Or, perhaps they saw themselves as *rejected*, either because they were experiencing poverty or had gained wealth or for another reason which created a division between them and other members of the family.

Money, as well as knowledge and sexuality, can create divisions among us. For the disciples on this first mission, setting aside their money was an important part of their mission strategy. Without monetary support, hospitality from those estranged members of the family was essential. The warm and generous hospitality they received from *the lost sheep of the house of Israel* was an unexpected and pleasant surprise.

LUKE 22:35

Hospitality opened the door for reconciliation. The disciples lived with the *lost* within the intimacy of their own homes. In this setting, *good news* could be shared and received with joy. Both those who brought the *good news* and those who received it could enjoy being together within their family of faith.

RELATED NOTES AND OBSERVATIONS

[C-13] MINISTRY WITHOUT MONEY

RELATED NOTES AND OBSERVATIONS

Personal Notes and Observations
reflecting on your own ministry without money.

A few questions to prompt questions of your own related to your faith journey.

Have there been times when your own faith journey was strengthened by unexpected hospitality from a neighbor or a member of your congregation?

OUR HEAVENLY FATHER CAME TO US WITH UNEXPECTED HOSPITALITY WHEN WE WERE BAPTIZED, ADOPTING US AS HIS CHILDREN, SEALING US WITH THE HOLY SPIRIT, AND MARKING US WITH THE CROSS OF CHRIST FOREVER.

Do you believe that this ministry of hospitality can transform lives by the power of the Gospel?

Is this ministry most important when there is a need for reconciliation with another person?

===

[C-13] MINISTRY WITHOUT MINISTRY

Congregational Notes and Observations reflecting your congregation's ministry without money.

A few questions to prompt questions of your own related to your congregation's ministries.

Is your congregation noted in your community for its hospitality toward everyone?

Are there people in your community who believe that your congregation would never welcome them?

Would members of your congregation have the courage to reach out to these people?

Do you think it might be possible that these members would experience unexpected hospitality?

HOW WOULD YOU ILLUSTRATE THE DIFFERENCES BETWEEN HOSPITALITY AND UNEXPECTED HOSPITALITY?

[C-14]

LOOKING BEYOND THE OBVIOUS

RELATED NOTES AND OBSERVATIONS

... the cares of the world and the lure of wealth choke the word and it yields nothing. ...

MATTHEW 13:22
CONTEXT: MATTHEW 13:1-53
SEE ALSO: MARK 4:1-34 AND LUKE 8:1-15

On this journey through the Gospels, it is important to look beyond the obvious. The specific text with which we begin this chapter obviously deals with money, but as we look beyond *the cares of this world and the lure of wealth,* we are confronted by the overwhelming reality of *the kingdom of heaven.*

We are aware that *the kingdom of heaven* is the central theme of the ministry of Jesus. He enlarges on this theme through his parables and his miracles. This 13th chapter of Matthew contains seven parables, each providing its own insight into *the kingdom of heaven.* This is a good time to review how we are to interpret parables.

MATTHEW 13:1-9, 24-53

Parables can be perplexing. The basic purpose of a parable is to enlighten the listener by conveying a great truth through everyday illustrations. A parable may also serve as a proverb which portrays dark truths about some of the listeners, making it embarrassing for them to accept what is being taught. While parables focus on a single truth, sometimes that truth may be enhanced through allegorical interpretations. When such interpretations are not provided in Scripture, the prudent reader will be content to reflect on the central truth revealed in the parable.

THE HEBREW WORD FOR *PARABLE* MEANS *A PROVERB. A THEOLOGICAL WORD BOOK OF THE BIBLE,*
P. 162
SEE ALSO MARK 3:23-27

MATTHEW 13:18-23, 35-43

The first parable in this chapter is an unforgettable story. If we miss the humor of it, we may also miss the point. In Palestine during the first century, seed was sown <u>before</u> the field was plowed. Then, as now, good seed was scarce; therefore, it was precious. While the sower would broadcast the seed with his hands to cover the field to be sown, care would be taken not to go beyond the boundaries of that field.

MATTHEW 13:1-9

In this parable, the sower throws seed everywhere — on the path, over rocky ground, among the thorns, beyond the boundaries, as well as into the fields. There must have been more than a few smiles on the faces of the listeners who could scarcely imagine a sower scattering expensive seed with such careless abandon.

Untold numbers of persons in that crowd may have gone home that day with only a rather silly story to tell. How could anyone take Jesus seriously when he didn't even use good sense concerning how to sow costly seed?

There would be others who would smile, and then wonder about the point of this parable concerning *the kingdom of God. When he (Jesus) was alone, those who were around him along with the twelve asked him about the parable.*

MARK 4:10

Jesus reminded them of the use of parable as proverb. In that large crowd, people listened at different levels to the story they heard. Some were simply following the crowd, expecting to be entertained. Some were hostile, hoping that Jesus would say something which they could use against him. Others were so caught up in *the cares of this world,* they heard little of what had been said.

MATTHEW 13:18-23

MATTHEW 21:28-44 RECORDS A SERIES OF PARABLES/ PROVERBS WHICH THE PHARISEES HEARD AS DIRECTED AT THEM. SEE MATTHEW 21:45-46

As we reflect on the meaning of this parable, behind the humor we see the central truth which we discovered in earlier chapters. The kingdom of God is characterized by abundance, not scarcity.

The seed of the word is scattered everywhere, not only among people who are eager and able to hear it. It is offered freely to everyone again and again.

Looking beyond the obvious, we ponder the awesome truth that Jesus is the Word. *In the beginning was the Word, and the Word was with God and the Word was God. . . . All things came into being through him . . . And the Word became flesh and lived among us . . . full of grace and truth. The Word became flesh* in the life of Jesus who shares his creative word, *full of grace and truth,* throughout the world.

IN THIS PASSAGE *WORD* IS CAPITALIZED FOR IT REFERS TO A PHILOSOPHICAL CONCEPT CONCERNING CREATION. THE SAME GREEK WORD, *LOGOS,* USED IN THIS PASSAGE IS ALSO USED IN THIS PARABLE.

JOHN 1:1,3,14

His word has transforming power. It is shared with those who are not particularly interested and quickly forget what they have heard. It is shared with others who respond with enthusiasm but there is no depth to their commitment. And, it is shared with persons who are so busy with their own affairs, they have no interest in having their lives taken in a new direction.

Over the centuries, this creative word continues to be sown among people of every race and nation. For some fortunate folks, the seed of God's word begins to take root early in their lives. They may go through various times when, for a variety of reasons, they are tested and their faith becomes fragile. Yet, in the main, their commitment to Christ is an abiding reality which shapes their attitudes and actions.

The faith journey of some other folks will be far more difficult. They may remain within the church for the circumstances of their life make it easier to worship with some regularity than to admit to their own lack of commitment to Christ. Others will wander away, exploring other options, searching for meaning through other avenues, or they are simply distracted by *the cares of this world and the lure of wealth.*

The Word continues to give himself freely to everyone everywhere. The commitment of Christ took him to a cross. His word, empowered by his sacrifice, makes it possible for us to be forgiven and welcomed into his kingdom. His kingdom is both a present and a future reality. The Church is a sign of his kingdom now. At the end of the age, Christ will come again to welcome us into his eternal kingdom.

In *The Parable of the Weeds and the Wheat,* we are reminded that his kingdom now is far from perfect. Within the faith community, the devil continues to be active, sowing *weeds* among the *wheat.* Christ does not want his people to become judge and jury, claiming for themselves the mission to identify the enemies in their midst and to drive them out. We run the risk of uprooting the *wheat* as well as the *weeds.*

RELATED NOTES AND OBSERVATIONS

MATTHEW 13:23

MATTHEW 13:22

MATTHEW 13:24-42

IT IS WELL TO REMEMBER THE EXPERIENCE OF THE CHURCH IN GERMANY DURING HITLER'S EVIL DICTATORSHIP.
SEE *A QUIET REFORMER; EDMUND SCHLINK'S LIFE* BY EUGENE M. SKIBBE

In his kingdom now, imperfect as it is, the transforming word continues to be sown with confidence that its power can defeat the enemy so that *weeds* become *wheat.* The history of the Church is filled with stories about its enemies who have become its advocates. *Therefore, do not pronounced judgment before the time, before the Lord comes, who will bring to light the things now hidden in darkness and will disclose the purposes of the heart.*

SAUL WHO BECAME PAUL IS AN OUTSTANDING EXAMPLE.

I CORINTHIANS 4:5

The transforming power of the word at work within the kingdom is illustrated in various ways by *The Parable of the Mustard Seed* and *The Parable of the Yeast.* For those who have experienced its power, the *kingdom of heaven is like a treasure,* or *like finding a pearl of great price,* but always, this kingdom now, *is like a net that was thrown into the sea, and caught fish of every kind.*

MATTHEW 13:44
MATTHEW 13:45-46

MATTHEW 13:47-50

From the perspective of money, our attention returns to those *who hear the word, but the cares of this world and the lure of wealth choke the word, and it yields nothing.* In this present time, their numbers are legion. Some of them have been captured by greed, but not all of them, and it is not our function to act as their judge.

MATTHEW 13:22

Many of them are burdened with anxiety lest their families be in want because they did not work hard enough. For others, the prospect of wealth is so attractive, they cannot imagine that money itself could rob them of the *true riches* to be found within the kingdom.

LUKE 16:11

A ministry to these people is like sowing seed *among thorns.* The presence of *thorns* suggests a variety of possibilities ranging from brambles to roses. These people may have surrounded themselves with prickly barriers or with extravagant luxuries but the thorns *choked* the seed, making growth difficult.

MATTHEW 13:7

Looking beyond the obvious, we are not to be discouraged. The metaphorical measure of the transforming power of the word is that the seed *brought forth grain, some a hundred-fold, some sixty, some thirty.* With God *all things are possible.*

MATTHEW 13:8

As we reflect on some of the specific changes which can take place among persons *in Christ*, we may discover that *the cares of this world* has been replaced by cares <u>for</u> this world. They begin exercising creative stewardship in behalf of the world which God loves so deeply.

The *lure of wealth* no longer determines the direction for their living. They have been set free to use wealth as a linchpin in a variety of constructive ways which honor Christ and facilitate ministries within their own neighborhoods and for the sake of persons in many distant places.

RELATED
NOTES AND OBSERVATIONS

JOHN 3:16

[C-14]   LOOKING BEYOND THE OBVIOUS

Personal Notes and Observations
    reflecting on *the cares of this world*.

A few questions to prompt questions of your own related to your faith journey.

Have there been times when *the cares of this world and the lure of wealth* made it difficult for you to hear and to live by the Gospel?

    MATTHEW 13:22

If this has been your experience, do you remember what it was that turned you around?

Have you had opportunities to be of help to someone for whom *the cares of this world and the lure of wealth* has made it difficult for them to hear the Gospel?

    AN IMPORTANT WITNESS OF OUR FAITH TO OUR FAMILY MEMBERS INVOLVES OUR FINANCIAL PLANNING AND PRIORITIES. HAVE YOU CONSIDERED MAKING PLANS FOR THE NEXT FIVE YEARS?

[C-14]   LOOKING BEYOND THE OBVIOUS

Congregational Notes and Observations
    reflecting of *the cares of this world*.

A few questions to prompt questions of your own related to your congregation's ministries.

In your judgment, do your congregation's yearly budgets appear to give greater emphasis to *the cares of this world* rather than proclaiming the Gospel?

Is your congregation bold enough to reach out with abandon to transform lives by the Gospel of grace? Does the congregation's budget allow this to happen?

Are there some specific goals you would want to appear in your congregation's mission plans over the next five years as an expression of its faith and its vision?

    BUILDING YEARLY BUDGETS FOR THE NEXT FIVE YEARS CAN LIFT THE VISION OF MEMBERS AS THEY ARE CONFRONTED WITH GOALS WHICH REFLECT THEIR FAITH.

RELATED NOTES AND OBSERVATIONS (margin heading)

[C-15]

LISTENING AT THE EDGES

RELATED
NOTES AND OBSERVATIONS

Six months wages would not buy enough bread for each of them to get a little.

JOHN 6:7
CONTEXT: JOHN 6:1-15
        MATTHEW 14:13-21
        MARK 6:30-44
        LUKE 9:10-17

Parables and miracles; illustrations and demonstrations; memorable words and extraordinary events: these are the means our Lord used to reveal himself and to make known the Kingdom of God. A monetary perspective prompts us to try *looking beyond the obvious* and to spend some time *listening at the edges.*

Giving attention to trivial things may prove helpful as we try *listening at the edges.* On this journey we have become accustomed to the brevity of Mark. We have expected a more complete account in Matthew. Time after time, we have turned to Luke for additional details. In this story of *The Feeding of the Five Thousand,* our expectations are turned upside down. Brevity is found in Luke. Matthew leaves out some interesting details. It is in Mark where the most complete account is to be found.

Also, for only the second time on this journey, we are confronted by a story which, in various ways, is found in all four Gospels. It is in the Gospel of John where, by *listening at the edges,* we discover details which make this miracle very personal for us as followers of Christ.

From a monetary perspective, we give our attention to a private conversation between Jesus and Philip. This conversation is not recorded in Matthew or in Luke. In Mark, the disciples ask Jesus, *Are we to go and buy two hundred denarii worth of bread and give it to them to eat?* In John's Gospel, it is Philip who is put to the test and it is Philip who responds, *Six months wages would not buy enough bread for each of them to get a little.*

MARK 6:37

JOHN 6:6
TWO HUNDRED DENARII
IS FREELY TRANSLATED
SIX MONTHS WAGES
TO SUGGEST THE VALUE
OF THIS MUCH MONEY.

73

Philip personifies the point of view which sees money as an essential linchpin to make ministry possible. If the necessary funds are not available, or if a particular ministry is deemed too expensive, then further discussion is futile.

Earlier, the disciples had suggested to Jesus that he send the crowd away so that they could secure food for themselves. Jesus said to them, *You give them something to eat.* The response of the disciples suggests that their treasury had the resources to make this humanitarian gesture possible. However, with pragmatic realism, Philip estimates that even spending all that silver would not accomplish a noteworthy purpose.

Listening at the edges, we remember the compassion Jesus had for this multitude who *were like sheep without a shepherd.* Compassion is not always practical. Further, we hear clearly that this monetary question was only a way our Lord used to test Philip *for he knew what he was going to do.* In our own time, as we are confronted by ministry possibilities which call for our compassion, it is often monetary considerations which put us to the test.

This is a good time to reflect on the meaning of miracles. In most of the New Testament, the Greek words used with reference to miracles are *dunameis* = power, and *terata* = wonder. In the Gospel of John, miracles are referred to as *semeia* = signs. Miracles are more than wonders which reflect the power of God. They are also signs which reveal who Jesus is, and which provide insights into the Kingdom of God.

Listening at the edges allows us to hear the conversation which Andrew had with a young boy. With child-like faith, this boy offered his food to satisfy the hunger of all the people who surrounded him. It was Andrew who was willing, in spite of its lack of logic, to make known this boy's offer to Jesus. *There is a boy here who has five barley loaves and two fish. But what are they among so many people?*

RELATED NOTES AND OBSERVATIONS

SEE MATTHEW 14:21 — *ABOUT FIVE THOUSAND MEN, BESIDES WOMEN AND CHILDREN.*

MARK 6:35-36

MARK 6:37

MARK 6:34

JOHN 6:6

THIS IS THE ROOT WORD FOR *DYNAMITE.*

IN THE RECENT PAST, SCIENCE CALLED INTO QUESTION THE POSSIBILITY OF MIRACLES. NOW SCIENTIFIC DISCOVERIES HAVE CREATED AN AGE OF MIRACLES.

WE REMEMBER OUR LORD'S RESPONSE WHEN HE WAS ASKED WHO IS THE GREATEST IN THE KINGDOM OF GOD — SEE MATTHEW 18:1-5.

JOHN 6:9

In that time and place, barley was fed to cattle. Only the poor would bake barley loaves for their family. Five barley loaves and two fish, a modest yet a sacrificial gift, was offered by a boy. The response of Jesus was simple and straightforward: *Make the people sit down.* So they all sat down on the grass which covered this large area. Mark indicates that the people sat down *in groups of hundreds and fifties.* Luke suggests that this grouping was ordered by Jesus.

What happened next is made clear in all four Gospels. *Taking the five loaves and two fish, he (Jesus) looked up to heaven, and blessed and broke the loaves, and gave them to his disciples to set before the people; and he divided the two fish among them all.*

You remember the rest of this story. The 12 disciples brought this food to that multitude. When the hunger of all those men, women, and children was satisfied, the disciples went and gathered up 12 baskets filled with the food that was left over.

Listening a the Edges now prompts us to consider the context of this amazing event. That evening the disciples got into a boat and started rowing across the sea back to Capernaum. Jesus was not with them. The sea became rough. Then *they saw Jesus walking on the sea ... and they were terrified. But he said, "It is I; do not be afraid.* Soon they reached Capernaum and again, the next day they were confronted by the people who had eaten the bread he had given them.

This was the miracle recorded in the first portion of the sixth chapter of John. In the closing portion of this chapter, Jesus says, *I am the living bread that came down from heaven. Whoever eats of this bread will live forever; and the bread that I will give for the life of the world is my flesh.*

The Feeding of the Five Thousand is an event of personal importance. We are led to reflect on the Kingdom of God where compassion is not restricted to tragedies. The first miracle (*semeia*) in John's Gospel simply saves a bridegroom in Cana from embarrassment at his wedding.

RELATED NOTES AND OBSERVATIONS

JOHN 6:10

MARK 6:40
LUKE 9:14

MATTHEW 14:19
LUKE 9:16
JOHN 6:11
MARK 6:41

JOHN 6:19-20

JOHN 6:23

JOHN 6:51

MATTHEW 4:4; JOHN 6:25-27

JOHN 2:1-11

In this miracle, our Lord's compassion only saves a night of discomfort for a great many people in need of an evening meal.

Further, within this defining moment of his ministry, Jesus chose to teach his followers concerning realities far more important than money. Through this miracle (*semeia*), Jesus reveals himself as God incarnate. Jesus said. *I am the bread that came down from heaven.*

On that day long ago, he looked out at a great multitude of men, women and children. Today, at this moment, he looks at you. He looks at each person around you, and at each person on the other side of the world. He does not measure your importance in monetary terms. We notice that all that silver played no part whatsoever in this miracle. Money was of secondary importance. In this event, the money is scarcely worth mentioning at all.

Jesus also makes his diety known in eucharistic language identifying bread and wine with his body and blood. He does so in language so specific they found it offensive. Consequently, *many of his disciples turned back and no longer followed him.* Our response would echo Peter's: *Lord, to whom shall we go? You have the words of eternal life. We have come to believe and know that you are the Holy One of God.*

RELATED NOTES AND OBSERVATIONS

OF COURSE, JESUS WAS QUICK TO SHOW COMPASSION WHEN FACED BY TRAGEDIES.
FOR EXAMPLE:
    MATTHEW 8:1-4
    MATTHEW 9:18-25
    MATTHEW 17:14-21

JOHN 6:41

JOHN 6:38-40

JOHN 6:54-57
JOHN'S GOSPEL DOES NOT INCLUDE AN ACCOUNT OF THE INSTITUTION OF THE LORD'S SUPPER.
JOHN 6:66

[C-15]   LISTENING AT THE EDGES   RELATED
                                                      NOTES AND OBSERVATIONS

Personal Notes and Observations
        related to tests involving finances and faith.

   *A few questions to prompt questions of your own
        related to your faith journey.*

   What monetary risks have you taken in order to carry out an act of compassion?

   Are you convinced that your giving plan for this year is a meaningful measure of your faith?

   Do you think it is appropriate to share your giving plan with your children?

===   =============================

[C-15]   LISTENING AT THE EDGES

Congregational Notes and Observations
        related to tests involving finances and faith.

   *A few questions to prompt questions of your own
        related to your congregation's ministries.*

   What risks do you think your congregation should be willing to take so that an act of compassion can take precedence over fiscal restraint?

   As you examine your congregation's spending plan for the coming year is it best to set a modest goal so that the congregation can be encouraged by success?

   Are there suggestions you want to share with your group with reference to taking a monetary risk as an act of faith?

DO YOU SEE
*THE FEEDING OF THE
FIVE THOUSAND* IN
TERMS OF UNEXPECTED
HOSPITALITY?
(SEE C-13)

77

[C-16]

LIFE AND LANGUAGE

*For what will it profit them
if they gain the whole world and forfeit their life?
Or what will they give in return for their life?*

    MATTHEW 16:26
CONTEXT: MATTHEW 16:24-26
SEE ALSO: MARK 8:34-37, AND
    LUKE 9:23-27

Reflections are rooted in language itself. Reflections on Gospel teachings are enriched by several languages: Aramaic, Greek and Hebrew together with modern languages. Personal reflections are so easily focused only on our mother tongue, the insights of other languages may be needed to broaden our horizons.

This chapter provides an opportunity for us to bring to mind lessons about language which we learned in years past. These insights will provide guidance as we reflect on this profound proclamation of our Lord.

We spoke our mother tongue before we learned to read and write. In the course of time, we discovered that what is meant by what is said is not limited by how our words are defined in a dictionary. The human voice can be used in many ways to give differing meanings to the words which are spoken.

FOR EXAMPLE, *HELLO* IS SIMPLY A SOCIAL NICITY UNLESS IT IS SHOUTED BY A PERSON WHO IS LOST. IT MAY ALSO SUGGEST A PERSON IS SURPRISED, OR SLEEPY, OR FLIRTATIOUS, OR CONFRONTATIONAL, ETC.

Similarly, how we speak can determine different meanings for words which have the same spelling. The voice may reveal whether the speaker is sick or healthy, drunk or sober, happy or sad. Even silence can speak in special ways, indicating shame, anger, or disappointment.

CONTRACT HAS ONE MEANING WHEN WE ACCENT THE FIRST SYLLABLE, AND ANOTHER WHEN WE EMPHASIZE THE SECOND SYLLABLE.

In addition, there is language which gets it meaning from our body. Body language may contradict our spoken language. Body language may convey one message in one culture and an opposite meaning in another culture. And, of course, a wink can have many meanings.

BODY LANGUAGE CAN INDICATE THAT *NO* IS REALLY *YES*. FOR US, AN UP-DOWN NOD MEANS *YES;* IN THE MIDDLE EAST IT MEANS *NO.* FOR US, SHAKING THE HEAD FROM SIDE-TO-SIDE MEANS *NO;* IN SOME ARAB COUNTRIES IT MEANS *YES.*

Everyone speaks with an accent. Judging by our accent, listeners may learn where we grew up in the U.S., or our accent may reveal our homeland in Europe, or Asia, or Africa, or Australia, or South America. Persons who learn English after they became adults may continue to think in the language of their childhood.

ENGLISH IS THE MOST WIDELY SPOKEN LANGUAGE IN THE WORLD. IT IS THE INTERNATIONAL LANGUAGE FOR SCIENCE AND TECHNOLOGY, AND IS USED THROUGHOUT THE WORLD IN BUSINESS AND DIPLOMACY. *ARTICLE ON ENGLISH LANGUAGE, WORLD BOOK ENCYCLOPDIA.*

In the 1st century, the people of Palestine spoke Aramaic which, like Hebrew, is a Semitic language. Aramaic had been the mother tongue in Palestine since about the 4th century B.C. Jesus and his disciples spoke Aramaic but they read their Bible in Hebrew which was the primary language of faith for the Jews. Greek was the international language of that day so this was the language in which the New Testament was written.

Thus far, the major texts for these chapters have been taken primarily from Matthew, Mark, and Luke. Our reflections on language provide some insights pertaining to the Greek style used in these three Gospels. *Mark's Greek is rough, strongly Aramaic, and often faulty, but it is fresh and frank. Matthew's Greek is also rather Aramaic, but smoother and more correct than Mark's. Luke's style is variable; excellent when he is writing independently but at other times incorporating the peculiarities of his sources.*

These stylistic differences remind us that the Bible is a human as well as a divine creation. It is the Word of God. It was written by men whose humanness is revealed in various ways.

These reflections on language can help us to focus on the pivotal teaching of Jesus which confronts us in this chapter. In each of the synoptic Gospels, this teaching is preceded by the confession of Peter, *You are the Messiah, the Son of the living God.* These Gospels go on to say in similar ways, *From that time on, Jesus began to show his disciples that he must go to Jerusalem and undergo great suffering . . . and be killed and on the third day be raised.*

Immediately following this pivotal teaching, each of these Gospels record what happened when Jesus took Peter, James and John with him up a high mountain and there he was transfigured before them.

The dramatic setting for this teaching encourages us to look closely at these three verses. It is not enough simply to read the words. Reflecting on the spoken message behind the words is our essential task.

The first verse is a summary of the way we are to walk as the people of God. *If any want to become my followers, let them deny themselves, and take up their cross and follow me.*

RELATED NOTES AND OBSERVATIONS

ARABIC AND A LANGUAGE SPOKEN IN ETHIOPIA CALLED *AMHARIC* ARE ALSO SEMITIC LANGUAGES. *ARAMAIC* IS STILL SPOKEN BY SOME ASSYRIAN CHRISTIANS.
ARTICLE ON SEMITIC LANGUAGES, WORLD BOOK ENCYCLOPIA.

GREEK BECAME THE STANDARD LANGUAGE OF THE MEDITERRANEAN COUNTRIES DURING THE DAYS OF ALEXANDER THE GREAT. EVEN AFTER THE RISE OF ROME, GREEK REMAINED THE PREFERRED LANGUAGE THROUGHOUT THE EMPIRE.

INTRODUCTION TO THE SYNOPTIC GOSPELS, AN ARTICLE IN THE JERUSALEM BIBLE.

CHAPTER #15 INCLUDES AN EMPHASIS ON THE GOSPEL OF JOHN.

MATTHEW 16:16, SEE ALSO MARK 8:29 AND LUKE 9:20.

MATTHEW 16:21, SEE ALSO MARK 8: 31 AND LUKE 9:21.

MATTHEW 17:1-8, SEE ALSO MARK 9:2-13 AND LUKE 9:28-36.

MATTHEW 16:24, SEE ALSO MARK 8:34 AND LUKE 9:23.

His disciples followed him, and came to the awesome conviction that Jesus of Nazareth was *the Messiah, the Son of the living God! Six days later* three of his disciples followed him up a mountain and were *eyewitnesses of his majesty.*

The second verse is a paradox; a statement which seems to be contradictory, but further reflection reveals a profound truth. *For those who want to save their life will lose it, and those who lose their life for my sake will find it.* How can we save something by losing it?

The third verse uses financial language plus rhetorical questions to underscore the great value of life. *For what will it profit them if they gain the whole world but forfeit their life? Or what will they give in return for their life?* Reflections on language remind us of the many faceted meanings of the word *life.*

The Hebrew word *ruach* means *wind* and *breath.* It takes us back to the basic meaning of *life* as the Creator God *breathed into his nostrils the breath of life, and man became a living being.* The Hebrew word for *wind* and *breath* also means *spirit* and *soul.* Neither Greek nor Hebrew draw a distinction between *soul* and *life.*

In the 1st century as in the 21st, *life* was and is understood as more than survival. To *have a life* involves success, and success was and is often measured in financial terms. Jesus makes it clear that when life is measured only in these terms, even if we *gain the whole world,* we *lose life* itself.

We trivialize his teaching if we suggest that the struggle for survival is wrong, or that achieving success is wrong, or even that gaining wealth is wrong. He teaches us that those who follow him will find the full meaning of life through service in his Name.

A basic goal of these chapters is to provide a basis for further reflection. The direction you take will be uniquely your own, reflecting your life and your own faith journey. As a starting point, you may find it helpful to continue your reflections where we began, with language itself.

RELATED NOTES AND OBSERVATIONS

MATTHEW 17:1-8

2 PETER 1:16-18

A PARADOX IS *A TRUTH STANDING ON ITS HEAD, WAVING ITS LEGS TO ATTRACT OUR ATTENTION. THE DOWNWARD ASCENT,* EDNA HONG, p. 16
MATTHEW 16:25, SEE ALSO MARK 8:35 AND LUKE 9:24.

MATTHEW 16:26, SEE ALSO MARK 8:36-37 AND LUKE 9:25.

THE KING JAMES VERSION USES THE WORD *SOUL* IN PLACE OF *LIFE.*

GENESIS 2:7

Accepted truisms within language are not always true, standing the test of careful examination. One of these truisms states boldly, *Money may not be of primary importance, but it is certainly a close second to whatever is first.*

It can be a helpful exercise to list all the things which are far more important to us than our money. Life itself will be on that list, together with family, faith, freedom, friends, our system of values, and our personal integrity. Where money does appear on this list, its importance is recognized. Money, as a human invention, remains a useful tool which can enable us, among other things, to pay for our children's education.

Further reflection brings to mind experiences which have taught us that less rather than more money can teach us what is worthwhile about life itself. More money can provide us with many things. Less money teaches us that the most important things in life are not things. Yet, again in this context, our reflections can affirm the importance of money.

In this chapter, three verses from the teachings of Jesus provided the focus for our reflections. First, Jesus spoke about the way we are to walk as his followers. Then he shares with us a paradoxical truth. Finally, using money as a metaphor, he affirms the importance of our lives. Ultimately, as we pursue our own reflections, we are drawn to what Jesus taught us about himself: *I am the way, and the truth, and the life.*

RELATED NOTES AND OBSERVATIONS

JOHN 14:6

[C-16]   LIFE AND LANGUAGE   RELATED
                                              NOTES AND OBSERVATIONS

Personal Notes and Observations
   on the role of language in your life of faith.

*A few questions to prompt questions of your own
   related to your faith journey.*

If you are entrusted with a family, are there some specific ways in which you make it clear to your children that money is of SECONDARY importance in your family?

Are there some specific ways through which your children discover that money which is shared is of secondary IMPORTANCE for our family of faith around the world?

As a family, does your giving become a source of joy in your living?

==
[C-16]   LIFE AND LANGUAGE

Congregational Notes and Observations
   on the role of language in your congregation's life.

*A few questions to prompt questions of your own
   related to your congregation's ministries.*

Does your congregation's stewardship ministry remind contributors that money is of SECONDARY importance; that why they give is of primary importance?

Are contributors also aware of the secondary IMPORTANCE of their monetary gifts as it is used to achieve goals of primary importance?

In what specific ways does your congregation celebrate the monetary gifts they receive from their members by sharing the joy it has brought to our family of faith around the world?

[C-17]

MONEY AND POWER

RELATED NOTES AND OBSERVATIONS

... 10,000 talents ... 100 denarii ...
Should you not have had mercy on your fellow servant as
I had mercy on you?

MATTHEW 18:24,28,33
CONTEXT:
MATTHEW 18:23-35

From the beginning we recognized that Jesus spoke often about money. He did so within the context of more important concerns. The importance of reflecting on Gospel teachings from the perspective of money is apparent.

The basic message of this parable is that God's mercy toward us is so great even a huge amount of money provides a poor comparison. Having experienced God's mercy, we are to forgive others as we have been forgiven.

THIS PARABLE IS FOUND ONLY IN MATTHEW'S GOSPEL.

As we reflect on this story from a monetary point of view, we see ourselves more clearly. We discover why it can be difficult for us to forgive others. We also discover why it can be difficult for us to accept God's forgiving mercy toward us.

We begin by noting the context. Jesus introduced this parable with the words, *For this reason . . . .* This phrase draws our attention to his teaching concerning the church which immediately precedes the telling of this parable. *If another member of the church sins against you, go and point out the fault when the two of you are alone.* This teaching includes the process to be followed in righting wrongs between members, together with the passage known as the *Keys of the Kingdom.* It concludes with the promise, *For where two or three are gathered in my name, I am there among them.*

MATTHEW 18:23

MATTHEW 18:15

MATTHEW 18:15-17

MATTHEW 18:18

MATTHEW 18:20

Then Peter asks Jesus, *Lord, if another member of the church sins against me, how often shall I forgive him? As many as seven times?* Jesus replied, *Not seven times, but, I tell you, seventy-seven times.*

MATTHEW 18:21

MATTHEW 18:22

83

Like many other parables, this story illustrates the *kingdom of heaven*. The main characters in this story are a *king* and *two slaves*. The Greek word for *slaves* can also be translated *servants*. We will follow the NRSV and its translation, *slaves*.

RSV AND KJV TRANSLATION IS *SERVANTS*.

The first slave worked for the king. The king discovered that he owed him *10,000 talents*. The RSV, which was translated in 1946, suggests that a *talent* was worth about $1,000. The NRSV was translated in 1989, and suggests that a *talent* was worth more than fifteen years' wages for a laborer.

RSV — THE KING WAS OWED $10 MILLION.

NRSV — IT WOULD TAKE A SLAVE 150,000 YEARS TO REPAY THE KING.

The second slave may or may not have worked for the king. He is simply called a *fellow slave*. He owed the first slave *100 denarii*. The NRSV estimates that a denarius was the usual day's wages for a laborer.

RSV SUGGESTS HE OWED ABOUT $20.
NRSV SUGGESTS HE OWED ABOUT ONE-THIRD OF A YEAR'S WAGES.

The first slave said to the king, *Have patience with me, and I wll pay your everything*. At first glance, this promise sounds preposterous. The second slave said to his fellow slave, *Have patience with me, and I will pay you*. This promise was within the realm of possibility.

MATTHEW 18:26

MATTHEW 18:29

In the *kingdom of heaven*, forgiveness is freely available to us because our Lord has paid an awesome price on our behalf. We do not merit the forgiveness we have received. In response to God's grace, we are to forgive as we have been forgiven. The question remains, Why is this so hard for us? In this parable, an answer to that question becomes available as we reflect on this story from the perspective of money.

It was within the realm of possibility for a slave in the 1st century to be held accountable by a king for a huge indebtedness. Kings would recognize the particular gifts of their slaves and assign them responsibilities accordingly.

JOSEPH WAS SOLD INTO SLAVERY BUT ACHIEVED A POSITION OF GREAT POWER UNDER THE PHARAOH, SEE GENESIS 39 AND FOLLOWING.

A slave who had the ability to invest large amounts of money profitably in behalf of the king would be given this power. Big returns require large risks. Even the most skilled steward is going to make some poor investments, perhaps even a series of poor investments.

In this parable, the king *wished to settle accounts with his slaves.* One of the king's slaves had made some poor investments so that the king's net worth suffered a serious loss. He reacted angrily. He decided to sell the slave, his family, and his possessions. We may be confident that this slave's net worth would have done very little to lessen the king's loss.

When this slave knelt before the king and pleaded, *Have patience with me and I will pay you everything,* this was not an empty promise. He had made a lot of money for the king in the past. He had made some serious errors in the present. The slave was simply asking for time to prove to the king that his financial skills continued to be of value.

Out of pity for him, the lord of that slave released him and forgave him the debt. It is apparent that this slave did not see himself as a person to be pitied or as someone who needed to be forgiven. From his point of view, the king was simply affirming his importance and returning him to his position of power.

But that same slave, as he went out, came upon one of his fellow slaves who owed him a hundred denarii. We are not told how this debt was incurred. Perhaps the second slave was struggling to find a way out of poverty. Even among slaves, it was recognized that money means power and power has its privileges.

Poverty has few privileges. On that short list of privileges is a rare opportunity to offer a proposal to a fellow slave who has power. Perhaps this proposal was such that, if it worked out, both slaves would one day have a nest egg which could open for them the door to freedom. However, this scheme proved to be just another failure. *Then his fellow slave fell down and pleaded with him, 'Have patience with me, and I will repay you.'*

The first slave was in no mood to have pity on his fellow slave, and he certainly did not want to forgive him. *He went and threw him in prison until he would pay his debt.* From his position of power, the first slave was convinced there was no excuse for his fellow slave to have failed. He was confident that the only reasonable thing to do was to confine his fellow slave within a debtor's prison.

RELATED NOTES AND OBSERVATIONS
MATTHEW 18:23

MATTHEW 18:26

MATTHEW 18:27

MATTHEW 18:28

MATTHEW 18:29

MATTHEW 18:30

As we look back to the 1st century and then look forward in this 21st century, the financial world remains remarkably the same. The power of money remains, together with its privileges. Poverty continues to have little power and few privileges. Wealthy countries must not be allowed to suffer economic ruin for that would be a threat to other wealthy countries. Wealthy persons have the power to influence national policies toward the goals of protecting and enhancing their net worth.

People of privilege see little need for personal forgiveness. At the same time, they may find it easy to see the poor as a national liability. Poverty is not to be forgiven, nor pitied. That only encourages the poor to expect more hand-outs from the wealthy.

In an earlier chapter, we considered the evidence that the financial world is changing. As we move into the 21st century, money will no longer be the decisive core of the financial world. Yet, at the personal level, how we use the money we have remains a decisive factor in the shaping of our character.

Within the community of God's people, forgiveness is offered freely both to the rich and to the poor. On the surface, it may seem apparent that individuals at worship are receiving God's forgiving grace with gratitude. Beneath the surface, as some of these individuals reflect on their own lives, they may see little need for forgiveness.

Persons with an abundance of money may be captured by the arrogance of power. With the privileges of power, they may not feel constrained to be forgiving toward the less fortunate.

Persons with little money may be convinced that their poverty offers the privilege to do whatever it takes to gain wealth. This leaves them with little interest to be forgiving toward anyone who may get in their way.

For every person within the community of God's people, one of the basic ways to discover whether we have accepted God's forgiving grace is to reflect on how freely we forgive others who owe us. This discipline lies at the core of our faith. It is one of the petitions within the prayer our Lord taught us.

RELATED NOTES AND OBSERVATIONS

MONEY AND CLASS IN AMERICA, P. 101-110

POST-CAPITALIST SOCIETY, P. 6

FORGIVE US OUR DEBTS, AS WE ALSO FORGIVE OUR DEBTORS. MATTHEW 6:12

[C-17]   MONEY AND POWER

Personal Notes and Observations reflecting on
   the power of money and the price of forgiveness.

*A few questions to prompt questions of your own
   related to your faith journey.*

   As a person of wealth, knowing that God's forgiving grace is of far greater value than your wealth, how do you live out this truth as a part of your faith journey?

   If you lost your wealth, knowing that God's forgiving grace is more important than your poverty, how would you live out this truth as a part of your faith journey?

   As a person of wealth, how are you indebted to the poor, and how can you forgive the debts they owe to you?

==

[C-17]   MONEY AND POWER

Congregational Notes and Observations reflecting on
   the power of money and the price of forgiveness.

*A few questions to prompt questions of your own
   related to your congregation's ministries.*

   When you confess your sins and then hear again the proclamation of the forgiveness of your sins is this a powerful experience for you?

   What can your congregation do to keep members alert and impressed by the power of Gospel truths which are repeatedly a part of their worship experience?

   In your judgment can the power of money be used to reveal to the wealthy and to the impoverished the price of God's forgiving grace?

[C-18]

WEALTH: A WORRISOME WONDER

Truly, I tell you, it will be hard for a rich person to enter the kingdom of heaven.

We are confronted with two stories. The first story is about a rich young man. The second story is about us as persons of wealth.

The rich young man is introduced simply as *someone*. In the middle of this story we are told that he was *young*. His story concludes with the information that *he had many possessions*.

The language of stories in the Gospels is noted for its sparcity. Consequently, every detail is significant. The simple detail that this rich man was introduced as *someone* suggests that he had not yet earned a name for himself.

In other encounters which Jesus had with rich persons, they were introduced by name: Matthew, Zacchaeus, Joseph of Arimathea, Nicodemus and so on. There were also women of wealth who provided financial support for the ministry of Jesus: Mary Magdalene, Joanna, Susanna, and others.

The *someone* in this story is also identified as *young*. A young man in our day may be someone between 18 and 35 years of age. Remembering the brevity of the span of life in Jesus' day, *young* suggests a person in his late teens or early twenties. The wonder of wealth may have surrounded his whole life. His many possessions became a key reality which identified how he saw himself.

As he approached adult responsibility for his good fortune, his wealth became worrisome. *Teacher, what good deed must I do to have eternal life?* Most wealthy families were followers of the Sadducees, the priests who were given positions of power by the Romans. The Sadducees rejected the teachings of Jesus concerning eternal life.

RELATED NOTES AND OBSERVATIONS

MATTHEW 19:23

CONTEXT: MATTHEW 19:16-26
SEE ALSO: MARK 10:17-31
AND LUKE 18:18-30

MATTHEW 19:16
MATTHEW 19:20
MATTHEW 19:22

SOCIAL RITUALS AND SMALL TALK ARE ABSENT.
CHRIST: A CRISIS IN THE LIFE OF GOD
BY JACK MILES. HE STRESSES THE SIGNIFICANT IMPORTANCE OF EACH RECORDED DETAIL.

MATTHEW 9:9; LUKE 19:1-10; JOHN 3:1-10, 19:38-40

LUKE 8:1-3

IN LUKE'S GOSPEL, HE IS IDENTIFIED AS A *CERTAIN RULER* SUGGESTING THAT HIS RICHES AND HIS MANY POSSESSIONS WERE LINKED WITH A HEREDITARY POSITION OF POWER.

MATTHEW 22:23-33

That *young someone* was well known to Jesus. As God incarnate, Jesus knew him better than that young man knew himself. He knew what prompted that question and he knew the more fundamental concerns hidden behind that question. Further, he was able to help this rich young man face his wealth as a worrisome wonder.

Why do you ask me about what is good? There is only one who is good. Only God is good. Good deeds in God's eyes are characterized by kindness, not by cost.

If you wish to enter into life, keep the commandments. Before we can consider eternal life, we must enter into life now. To enter life now in our own strength, we must keep the commandments. Obeying the commandments perfectly is not humanly possible.

Quickly sweeping aside the profound truths Jesus shared with him, this young man replied, *Which one?* With infinite patience, Jesus listed several of the Ten Commandments, concluding with *You shall love your neighbor as yourself.* With the confidence that is common among young men he said, *I have kept all these.*

The heart of this story is found in these words: *what do I still lack?* That fundamental question from this young man reflects maturity beyond his years. His future now hangs in the balance. Jesus said to him, *If you wish to be perfect, go, sell your possessions, and give to the poor, and you will have treasure in heaven; then come, follow me.*

If you wish to be perfect . . . In the Old Testament, *to be perfect means to be whole or sound or true.* In the New Testament, to be perfect *is the acceptance of grace, which is always whole, complete, perfect, and in the strength of this encounter our life is lived.*

The rich young man encountered a man far richer and more powerful than he. *He was in the world, and the world came into being through him; yet the world did not know him. . . . But to all who received him, who believed in his name, he gave power to become children of God. . . . From his fullness we have all received grace upon grace.*

RELATED NOTES AND OBSERVATIONS

JOHN 1:1, 14

MATTHEW 19:17
MARK 10:18
MATTHEW 25:34-36,
MATTHEW 26: 6-13
MARK 14:3-9

MATTHEW 19:17

ROMANS 3:12

MATTHEW 19:18

MATTHEW 19:18-19
MATTHEW 22:39

MATTHEW 19:20

MATTHEW 19:20
MARK 10:21; LUKE 18:22

MATTHEW 19:21
THE WORDS *THE MONEY* ARE OMITTED HERE FOR THEY ARE NOT FOUND IN THE GREEK TEXT.

A THEOLOGICAL WORD BOOK OF THE BIBLE, EDITED BY ALAN RICHARDSON, P. 167.

JOHN 1:10, 12, 16

Go, sell your possessions, and give the money to the poor. As indicated earlier, the Greek text lacks *the money.* The translators chose to add these words also where this story is recorded in the Gospel of Mark and the Gospel of Luke. We will reflect on this detail as we share the second story about us as persons of wealth.

You will have treasure in heaven . . . At the center of our Lord's response to this rich man is the affirmation that life eternal is a rich reality that is open to him. Further, he goes on to offer this young man a whole new life in the immediate present.

Come, follow me. This personal invitation brings to mind the calling of the disciples. To the fishermen, Peter and Andrew, he said, *Follow me and I will make you fish for people.* Other fishermen, James and John, also responded to his personal invitation. To Matthew, the tax collector, Jesus said, *Follow me. And he got up and followed him.*

In the following chapter in Matthew Jesus tells his disciples that he is going to Jerusalem where he would be crucified and on the third day he would be raised. He also knew that Judas would betray him. Following our Lord's ascension the disciples chose Mattias to replace Judas as one of the twelve disciples.

If the rich young man had followed Jesus, a whole new life could have opened up for him. In Mark's account of this story, we are told that *Jesus, looking at him, loved him.* Could it be that Jesus had this young man in mind to become the 12th disciple? This *someone* who had not yet earned a name for himself would have become known and honored over the centuries.

Sadly, this first story closes the door to that possibility. *When the young man heard this word, he went away grieving, for he had many possessions.* The worrisome wonder of his great wealth robbed him of *the life that really is life.*

RELATED NOTES AND OBSERVATIONS

MATTHEW 19:21

THE TRANSLATORS OF THE *REVISED STANDARD VERSION* AND *THE NEW ENGLISH BIBLE* CHOSE NOT TO ADD THE WORDS *THE MONEY.*
MARK 10:21; LUKE 18:22

MATTHEW 19:21

MATTHEW 19:21

MATTHEW 4:18-24

MATTHEW 9:9

MATTHEW 20:18-19

MATTHEW 10:4

ACTS 1:23-26

MARK 10:21

MATTHEW 19:22

I TIMOTHY 6:17-19

The second story is about us as persons of wealth.

Truly I tell you, it will be hard for a rich person to enter the kingdom of heaven. Again I tell you, it is easier for a camel to go through the eye of a needle than for someone who is rich to enter the kingdom of God.

MATTHEW 19:23-24

Each one of us is *someone*. We may be *young* or our youth may be a part of the past, but we remain *someone* who has *many possessions*. For us, wealth is a worrisome wonder.

Americans tend to live in denial of their wealth. The only thing they wonder about is what it would be like to be really rich. The disciples of Jesus did not hide behind this kind of denial. When they heard what their Lord said about the rich young man, *they were greatly astounded, and said, "Then who can be saved?"*

MATTHEW 19:25

Further, Jesus did not deny that his disciples were among the rich for whom entrance into the kingdom was so difficult. In response to their question he said to them and to us, *For mortals it is impossible, but for God all things are possible.*

MATTHEW 19:25

Obviously, not everyone is rich. Vast multitudes of our neighbors on this small planet are poor. They live from hand to mouth, with meager shelters, little clothing and a short span of life. Many of these neighbors live in distant places, out of sight and too easily out of mind. Some live right around us, working diligently and yet homeless, clothed properly and yet vulnerable to poverty-related dangers each day. As our church follows faithfully the teachings of our Lord, the importance of the poor is readily apparent.

PLEASE NOTE,
A SPECIAL PLACE FOR THE POOR,
CHAPTER #7.

Each one of us is someone for whom wealth is a wonder and a worrisome thing. The question we bring to Jesus will be different from the concern of that rich man who lived 2000 years ago. Perhaps our question will be as basic as *Why do I have what I have?*

OUR STEWARDSHIP; MANAGING OUR ASSETS,
BY JOHN L. GOLV,
P. 20.

Further questions may flow from this one, reflecting our own heritage and experiences. Finally, we need to arrive at the concern expressed in the first story, *What do I still lack?* As this story is told in the Gospels of Mark and Luke, it is Jesus who raises this issue as he says to that young man, *You lack one thing.*

MARK 10:21, LUKE 18:22

It is important for us to go back to the beginning. The first story began with the question, *Teacher, what good deed must I do to have eternal life?* Our question would be phrased somewhat differently. We know that eternal life will be ours ONLY through utter dependence on the grace of God. We also know that we are *created in Christ Jesus for good works, which God prepared beforehand to be our way of life.*

Our story begins with the question, *Teacher, in response to the generosity of your grace, what good works would you have me do with the wealth you have entrusted to me?* Jesus tells us, *Go, sell your possessions and give (the money) to the poor, . . . then come, follow me.*

What makes this so hard, like *a camel to go through the eye of a needle,* is our human tendency to see our Lord's teaching as an obligation rather than an opportunity. The greater our wealth, the more we may feel obligated to be generous. We tend, however, to be generous within the limitations of readily available cash. Generosity involving the disposal of our personal possessions may be much more difficult. Like the rich young man in the first story, we may be possessed and therefore enslaved by our own possessions.

What do I still lack? . . . Go, sell your possessions. Our Lord does not say, *sell your possessions* immediately. In this teaching he opens the door to an opportunity which can make the wonder of our wealth less worrisome.

Give the money to the poor . . . In the early days of the church, *no one claimed private ownership of any possessions, . . . there was not a needy person among them.* This practice proved difficult to sustain. It dealt boldly with the financial pains of poverty but left untouched the deeper problems of the poor.

Give to the poor . . . There are times when the poor need our time and our talents more than they need our cash. Money given to provide housing, health care, educational and employment opportunities can deal with the deeper problems of the poor. We discover that the rich need the poor even as the poor need the rich. Both the rich and the poor have a word of grace to share. We become aware of the many ways in which the lives of the rich and the poor are interrelated to the benefit of the whole community.

RELATED NOTES AND OBSERVATIONS

EPHESIANS 2:8-9

EPHESIANS 2:10

MATTHEW 19:21

MATTHEW 19:24

SEE MARK 10:21 AND LUKE 18:22

MATTHEW 19:21

MATTHEW 19:21
ACTS 4:32, 34

MATTHEW 19:21

It will be hard for a rich person to enter the kingdom of heaven . . . Within the wonder of our wealth, it is hard for us to see our own poverty. Perhaps the rich young ruler in the first story can provide a mirror for us. It is not difficult to see the depth of his poverty as he *went away grieving, for he had many possessions.* We are equally poor when we cling to our possessions as though they are of more value than the saving grace of God.

Come, follow me . . . As we follow him, encountering the grandeur of his grace through what he taught and what he did, we gain new insights as to how we can give creatively. His saving grace is measured, *not with silver or gold, but with his holy and precious blood and his innocent suffering and death. All this he had done that I may be his own, live under him in his kingdom, and serve him* . . . For rich persons like us, we can be his own, and live in his kingdom for with *God all things are possible.*

RELATED NOTES AND OBSERVATIONS

MATTHEW 19:23

LUKE 18:18

MATTHEW 19:22

MATTHEW 19:21

SEE LUKE 18:25-33
THE SMALL CATECHISM,
BY MARTIN LUTHER,
THE MEANING TO THE 2ND
ARTICLE OF THE CREED.

MATTHEW 19:26

[C-18] WEALTH: A WORRISOME WONDER

RELATED NOTES AND OBSERVATIONS

Personal Notes and Observations
    related to wealth, its worries and its wonders.

A few questions to prompt questions of your own related to your faith journey.

Accepting the level of wealth entrusted to your care, what worries come to your mind?

As you measure your wealth with reference to persons who are poor, what wonders come to your mind?

AS A MIDDLE CLASS AMERICAN, IF YOU ARE NOT CONVINCED THAT YOU ARE RICH, YOU ARE INVITED TO LOOK AHEAD AND READ CHAPTER #23, *RICH MAN, POOR MAN.*

What have you learned about wealth that you want to share with your children and your grandchildren?

If you are or were poor, what have you learned about poverty that you want to share with your children and your grandchildren?

===

[C-19] WEALTH: A WORRISOME WONDER

Congregational Notes and Observations
    related to wealth, its worries and its wonders.

A few questions to prompt questions of your own related to your congregation's ministries.

As you evaluate your congregation do you see it as rich or poor in monetary terms?

If you are convinced that your congregation is not poor, what can your group do to help your church accept its wealth and celebrate this reality?

As a member of a wealthy congregation, what worries and wonders occupy your mind?

[C-19]

GENEROSITY: HIS AND OURS

Am I not allowed to do what I choose with what belongs to me? Or are you envious because I am generous?

    This is an astonishing and familiar parable. When we hear the opening sentence — *For the kingdom of heaven is like a landowner who went out early in the morning to hire laborers for his vineyard* — we may easily remember the rest of the story.

    Some men were hired at 6 a.m.; others at 9 a.m. At noon and at mid-afternoon, and finally at just one hour before the end of the working day additional groups were invited to work in the vineyard.

    At the end of the day, this landowner instructed his steward to pay the men, beginning with those who had worked only one hour. Each man was to receive the same wage, the amount usually paid for 12 full hours of work.

    Those who had put in the most hours began to grumble. The landowner said to them, *Am I not allowed to do what I choose with what belongs to me? Or are you envious because I am generous?*

    The purpose of this astonishing parable is to affirm the personal worth of every individual. Jesus never met a person who was not important to him.

    He also sees each person in terms of their daily needs. Whether a worker had the opportunity to work 12 hours or only one hour, the reality remained that there were children at home who needed to be clothed and fed.

    Contemplating this parable, you are free to use your imagination. Have you ever wondered what happened on the next day, and the day after that, and on and on? You know that God's mercy, his gracious generosity. is *new every morning.*

\RELATED NOTES AND OBSERVATIONS

MATTHEW 20:15
CONTEXT: MATTHEW 20:1-16

THIS PARABLE IS FOUND ONLY IN MATTHEW.

MATTHEW 20:1

MATTHEW 20:2-7

MATTHEW 20:8-9

MATTHEW 20:10-12

MATTHEW 20:15

MATTHEW 20:16

LAMENTATIONS 3:22-23

In your imagination concerning the next day, how many of those men showed up for work at 5 o'clock in the afternoon? Perhaps there were some anxious souls whose first concern was to feed the family. They did not dare believe that the landowner's generosity would continue for two days in a row. They were ready for work at 6 a.m.

Others did not want to press their luck. They showed up at mid-morning. Yet others considered working half-a-day for a full day's pay to be good enough for them. Finally, there were the risk takers who waited until 3 p.m. or even until 5 p.m. to see if the landowner would be there to invite them to work. He was there.

At the end of "day two" everyone was given the same wage and those who had worked only one hour were paid first. If you were a part of this story which reveals God's gracious generosity, at what time during the next day would you show up for work?

Perhaps you choose to see this parable simply as an ancient fairy tale. In your experience, there is nothing like this in the real world so there is no purpose to saying more about it. Or you may see in this parable a fundamental truth which has shaped your living. God's gracious generosity has transformed your life.

As the days come and go, within your imagination, you begin to see a pattern developing. In general terms, you see that about 50% of the people go to work in the vineyard in mid-afternoon or at the very last hour. Another 20% have gotten into the habit of arriving at noon, working a half-day. About 15% are at work every morning at 9 a.m., and the remaining 15% are eager to work the full 12 hour day.

Unfortunately, the passing days also reveal a sizeable number of persons who simply refuse to work in the Lord's vineyard. They are, indeed, *envious of his generosity.* They want to make money the old-fashioned way: they want to earn it by their own efforts.

When God's gracious generosity has transformed our lives, then this ancient parable is turned up-side down.

RELATED NOTES AND OBSERVATIONS

AS WE IMAGINE WHAT MAY HAVE TAKEN PLACE ON SUBSEQUENT DAYS, WE MAY BRING TO MIND ANOTHER TEACHING OF JESUS IN WHICH THE METAPHOR OF A VINEYARD IS USED.

SEE JOHN 15:1-11.

HERE CHRIST IS PORTRAYED AS THE VINE AND CHRISTIANS ARE PICTURED AS THE BRANCHS IN THE VINEYARD.

JOHN 15:5

JOHN 15:9

JOHN 15:11

MATTHEW 20:15

MATTHEW 20:15

In the parable that is familiar to us, it was the men who had worked the full 12 hour day who grumbled at the landowner's generosity. As this story has continued down to this present time, grumbling is rarely heard from the folks who come to work every morning.

Now the grumbling often comes from those who appear for work around noon and complain about those who work fewer hours than they. From their point of view, if everyone in the work force would each put in 5 or 6 hours a day, the basic work of the vineyard would be completed and no one would have to sacrifice too much of their time and their effort.

The most fascinating part of this continuing story centers in the lives of those who willingly do most of the work in the vineyard. The focus of their lives is not on how much work they do, but on the gracious generosity of him for whom they work.

It was his gracious generosity which set them free from daily anxiety about what they would eat, or what they would drink, or what they would wear. Their Lord knew they would need all these things.

As their value system changed, they, themselves, were transformed. They began to see themselves as persons of great worth for this is how they were treated. The owner of the vineyard dealt with them as his own brothers and sisters.

Now their primary mission in life is to help that vineyard to achieve its full potential. That goal is not simply to produce more and more grapes, but rather to work for the transformation of more and more lives through the gracious generosity which is offered freely to every person.

As the years pass by, the Lord's gracious generosity begins to be reflected in the lives of people eager to come to work every morning. It is often shown through warm, open, and honest hospitality toward their friends who come to work in the afternoon. They are delighted when new friends start to work, even if they do so at the last hour.

RELATED NOTES AND OBSERVATIONS

IT IS COMMONPLACE AMONG CONGREGATIONS IN OUR TIME FOR A SMALL PERCENTAGE OF ITS MEMBERS TO VOLUNTEER FOR THE TASKS WHICH REQUIRE THE MOST AMOUNT OF TIME. THEY ALSO PROVIDE MOST OF THE FINANCIAL RESOURCES NEEDED BY THE CONGREGATION TO MEET ITS MISSION GOALS.

SEE JOHN 15:12-17

MATTHEW 6:25-33

JOHN 15:13,14

JOHN 15:15

JOHN 15:16

They are understanding and patient with other friends who would like to enforce a sense of fairness by dividing the work equally among everyone. Their patience with this idea does not mean they agree with it. In this vineyard, it is not equal sacrifice but the gracious generosity of God which has transforming power.

His generosity prompts them to be generous with their time, their skills, and with the financial resources he has entrusted to their care. To follow Christ reflects their love, their faith, and their striving for justice throughout the earth.

In this continuing story over the centuries, multitudes of people bear witness that the generosity of their heavenly Father makes all of life rich and free.

RELATED NOTES AND OBSERVATIONS

[C-19]   GENEROSITY: HIS AND OURS   RELATED
                                           NOTES AND OBSERVATIONS

Personal Notes and Observations
    related to God's generosity toward us.

*A few questions to prompt questions of your own
    related to your faith journey.*

Would your faith journey be easier to manage if God's generosity did not trouble you?

As a person who gives generously to your church, would you be willing to give less if others gave more to meet the mission goals of the congregation?

Are some of your friends puzzled by your generosity? Has the IRS questioned your generosity?

===

[C-19]   GENEROSITY: HIS AND OURS

Congregational Notes and Observations
    related to God's generosity toward us.

*A few questions to prompt questions of your own
    related to your congregation's ministries.*

As you analyze your congregation, what percentage of the membership contributed most of the time and money needed to meet the congregation's goals?

If your congregation's stewardship ministry had as its primary focus the transforming power of God's generosity, would this be an effective way for your congregation to meet is mission goals?

DO YOU THINKS THAT THIS FOCUS WOULD ENLARGE THE PERCENTAGE OF MEMBERS WHO GIVE GENEROUSLY?

If you think that his focus has practical as well as spiritual potential, what idea will you want to share with your group?

[C-20]

PRAYERS OR PREYERS

RELATED
NOTES AND OBSERVATIONS

*'My house shall be called a house of prayer,
but you are making it a den of robbers.'*

MATTHEW 21:13
ISAIAH 56:7 — JEREMIAH 7:11

The story of the cleansing of the Temple is recorded in all four Gospels. In each Gospel we find very different versions of this story. It merits a moment of our time to review the details.

CONTEXT: MATTHEW 21:12-17
SEE ALSO: MARK 11:11. 15-19
LUKE 19:45-48
JOHN 2:13-22

1. In Matthew, after the triumphal entry into Jerusalem, Jesus cleanses the temple, and then goes to Bethany to spend the night there.

MATTHEW 21: 1-11
MATTHEW 21:17

2. In Mark, after the triumphal entry into Jerusalem, Jesus *went to the temple . . . Looked around at everything . . .* then went to Bethany. On the following day, he cleansed the temple.

MARK 11:11

3. In Luke, following the triumphal entry, our Lord had a confrontation with some Pharisees who objected to the welcome he had received. He foretold the destruction of Jerusalem, and then entered the temple to cleanse it.

LUKE 19:29-44

4. In John the timing of this event takes place toward the beginning of our Lord's ministry, not just few days before his death. Jesus does not foretell the destruction of Jerusalem but compares the temple to his own body.

JOHN 1:29, 35, 43, 2:1.

JOHN 2:18-22

Aren't the four Gospels biographies of the greatest life ever lived? If they are not biographies, what kind of literature are they?

At this point in our faith journey we may benefit by reflecting on these questions. Biographies give careful attention to chronology. The date of birth and the time of death provide the basic boundaries for a biography. However, the Gospels do not abide by those boundaries.

Again, it is time well spent to consider these differences.

1. Matthew begins with the genealogy of Jesus going back to Abraham, and devotes only one verse to his birth.

MATTHEW 1:1-17
MATTHEW 1:25

100

2. Mark begins with our Lord's baptism by John the Baptist. Jesus, as an adult, was at the beginning his ministry. He does not provide a genealogy of Jesus.
3. Luke begins with the birth of John the Baptist. Then the story of Mary and the birth of Jesus is told in great detail. Luke records the genealogy of Jesus going back all the way to Adam.
4. John goes back to the creation, telling the story of Jesus who *was in the world and the world came into being through him.*

RELATED NOTES AND OBSERVATIONS

MARK 1:1-4

LUKE 1:5-2:20

LUKE 3:23-38

JOHN 1:1-5
JOHN 1:10

The primary focus of the four Gospels goes beyond the death of Jesus to his resurrection. His resurrection sheds its miraculous light on everything which Jesus said and did during his life. Further, his resurrection sheds its miraculous light into the lives of individuals who live by faith in him throughout the following millennia.

The special purpose of the four Gospels is proclamation. With this in mind, our contemplation on the cleansing of the temple prompts us to consider some earlier events.

"THE CANONICAL GOSPELS ARE NOT...BIOGRAPHIES... THEY ARE NOT SIMPLY MEMOIRS OF A TEACHER, PHILOSOPHER OR WISE MAN ...THE GOSPELS REPRESENT A GENRE ALL THEIR OWN BECAUSE THEY PRESENT THE TRADITION OF JESUS FROM THE VIEWPOINT OF FAITH IN HIM AS REDEEMER. HENCE IT WAS THE INTENTION OF THE FOUR EVANGELISTS THAT THEIR GOSPELS BE UNDERSTOOD NOT ONLY AS NARRATIVE, BUT AT THE SAME TIME AND ESPECIALLY AS PROCLAMATION."
THE NEW OXFORD ANNOTATED BIBLE,
P. VIII NT - IX NT.

When Jesus was 12 years old, he went with his parents to the Passover festival in Jerusalem. What catches our attention is a question Jesus poses for his parents, *Did you not know that I must be in my Father's house?*

LUKE 2:41-51

LUKE 2:49

Years later in Capernaum, a temple tax collector asked Peter if Jesus paid this tax. When Peter and Jesus talked about this issue, they used the analogy of a king and his children, and concluded that the king's children would not pay taxes. *However,* said Jesus, *so that we do not give offense to them, go to the sea and cast a hook.* In the mouth of the fish a coin was found which was used to pay the temple tax both for Peter and Jesus.

MATTHEW 17:24

MATTHEW 17:25-28

Obviously, Jesus, the Son of God, had a unique relationship with the temple extending back over centuries of time. Turning *a house of prayer* into *a den of robbers* was deeply offensive to him, prompting his dramatic response.

ISAIAH 56:7 —
JEREMIAH 7:11

MATTHEW 21:13

As we move from the 1st century to the 21st, we ponder what our Lord's response will be toward the congregation to which we belong. We are reminded that *a congregation resembles three different institutions at the same time: a community of spiritual transformation, a voluntary association, and a non-profit organization.*

OUR STEWARDSHIP;
MANAGING OUR ASSETS,
JOHN L. GOLV, P. 8

This three-in-one characteristic is true of congregations which are old or new, large or small, rural or urban, and of differing denominations. Some congregations may be strong in one of these dimensions and weak in another.

Gifts from our heavenly Father become the assets of the congregation. As *a community of spiritual transformation*, our congregation's assets are the Word and Sacraments, the experience of our Lord's presence, and the guidance of the Holy Spirit.

Gifts from God are also the assets of the congregation as *a voluntary association*. Faith, hope, and love become assets within individual lives. Their witness draw others into a closer relationship with God. These assets are also at work beyond the congregation to serve the cause of justice and mercy for everyone, everywhere.

Gifts from God are assets of the congregation also as *a non-profit organization*. In this chapter, we will focus on this dimension of our congregation.

As a non-profit organization, a congregation is similar to a business that offers services to the public. Volunteers with gifts which are valued in the business world are assets within the congregation as they handle monetary matters, develop personnel policies, and care for its property.

A congregation is similar but not identical to a business. When Jesus cleansed the temple, he cried out, *Stop making my Father's house a marketplace!* As the disciples heard this, they remembered that it was written, *Zeal for your house has consumed me.*

JOHN 2;16

JOHN 2:17 — PSALM 69:9

102

His disciples did not see our Lord's words and actions as an outburst of temper, but *the energy of righteousness against the religious leaders to whom religion had become a business.*

Our Lord is offended when money is elevated above its proper place of SECONDARY importance. Prayer, praise, and proclamation lose their high priority. What we can afford, not our faith, determines the boundaries of our mission and ministry. As a congregation loses its vision, it also loses its vitality. It no longer functions effectively as *our Father's house.*

Money is a SECONDARY gift from God. We earn money when our primary gifts from God are valued in the world of commerce. As the people of God, money is evaluated as of secondary IMPORTANCE. Its importance prompts us to receive it with thanksgiving.

Money received with thanksgiving is also given with thanksgiving. Thanksgiving prompts us to measure, not simply the proportion of God's gifts to us which we return to him, but also the proportion which we retain with thanksgiving and over which we strive to practice good stewardship.

As we turn again to view our congregation as a great gift from God to us, we sense once more the splendor and majesty of *our Father's house.*

RELATED NOTES AND OBSERVATIONS

THE NEW OXFORD ANNOTATED BIBLE, P. 127 NT

SEE CHAPTER #13, *MINISTRY WITHOUT MONEY*

[C-20]   PRAYERS OR PREYERS   RELATED
                                                 NOTES AND OBSERVATIONS

Personal Notes and Observations
      related to our zeal for our church.

   *A few questions to prompt questions of your own
         related to your faith journey?*

Why is it important for you to worship each week?

You see the church as a *house of prayer;* others see it as a *den of robbers;* how can you assure them that they are mistaken?   MATTHEW 21:13

You see the church as our *Father's house;* how do you show reverence for this holy place?   LUKE 2:49

===

[C-20} PRAYERS OR PREYERS

Congregational Notes and Observations
      related to your zeal for your church.

   *A few questions to prompt questions of your own
         related to your congregation's ministries.*

What guidelines does your congregation follow to affirm the sanctity of your place of worship?

What guidelines are followed so that your community will not see your congregation as a non-profit, charitable business?

What guidelines have been developed to affirm for your members that faithful worship is of fundamental importance for them and for your congregation?

[C-21]

TAXES AND GIVING

Give therefore to the emperor the things that are the emperor's, and to God the things that are God's.

Reflecting on a Biblical text in terms of what it meant in the 1st century is a basic first step. Reflecting on a text in terms of what it means in the 21st century is the normative second step. Sometimes, following this routine procedure changes the focus of the text. NOW we are prompted to consider issues which were not considered THEN.

THEN the focus in this text was on a trap the Pharisees prepared to get Jesus in trouble. After a bit of flattery, they posed the question, *Is it lawful to pay taxes to the emperor, or not?*

In the 1st century the Roman emperor was the enemy. Palestine was one of many countries which the emperor had conquered. Obedience was demanded, including paying the taxes required of them.

On the one hand, if Jesus taught his countrymen not to pay these taxes he would quickly bring down upon himself the emperor's wrath.

On the other hand, approving the payment of these taxes would bring down upon him the wrath of his countrymen. Many of his followers saw Jesus as a prophet. A prophet without courage would be despised.

The Pharisees were confident that this approach would entrap Jesus. If he remained silent or if he said *yes* or if he said, *no:* none of these options would be satisfactory. Jesus was fully aware of their malice and called them *hypocrites*.

Very quickly, Jesus trapped them. He asked them to identify the head on the coin which was used to pay the tax.

RELATED
NOTES AND OBSERVATIONS

MATTHEW 22:21
CONTEXT:
    MATTHEW 22:15-22
SEE ALSO: MARK 12:13-17
    LUKE 20:20-26

MATTHEW 22:17

MATTHEW 22:18

The only answer they could give was to say that it was the emperor's head. If they suggested that his head on the coin did not mean they had to pay taxes to him, they would bring upon themselves his wrath.

Jesus went on to teach them, and us, a fundamental lesson. He said, *Give therefore to the emperor the things that are the emperor's, and to God the things that are God's.* We are told that when they heard this, *they were amazed,* and they left him and went away.

MATTHEW 22:21
MATTHEW 22:22

If they were amazed because Jesus had avoided their trap and laid a trap for them, then they were astonished for the wrong reason. Jesus was doing far more than avoiding their attempt at malicious mischief. He was affirming what he had taught since the beginning of his ministry.

In the Sermon on the Mount, he proclaimed, *You have heard that it was said, 'You shall love your neighbor and hate your enemy.' But I say to you, Love your enemies and pray for those who persecute you.* Our Lord practiced what he preached even when those who hated him crucified him. From the cross he prayed, *Father, forgive them; for they do not know what they are doing.*

MATTHEW 5:43-44

LUKE 23:34

That was THEN, this is NOW. As Americans, we are not ruled by a foreign enemy. Year after year we are involved in debates about taxes of one kind or another. We can and do voice varying opinions about these taxes but this does not call into question our love for our country.

We are free to <u>avoid</u> paying taxes which can legally be avoided. We will forfeit our freedom if we <u>evade</u> paying taxes which are legally binding upon us. A portion of what we earn in this free country must be paid in taxes so that we can benefit from the services which our government provides.

NOW the focus on this text moves from *Give therefore to the emperor the things that are the emperor's* to the second portion of this teaching where we are taught to give *to God the things that are God's.* The question now under consideration is *What things belong to God?*

MATTHEW 22:21

RELATED NOTES AND OBSERVATIONS

Pondering this question can be an amazing experience for us. A story from Paul's missionary journeys comes to mind. Paul's primary mission was to tell the story of Jesus; about his teachings and his miracles, and about his death and resurrection. Paul was also a fund-raiser, diligently raising money for the poor in Jerusalem.

In his 2nd letter to the Corinthians, Paul tells a story about the Macedonians. He did not tell this story to embarrass the Corinthians but to complement them. It is not our purpose to emphasize the poverty of those Macedonians.

We are reflecting on the teaching of Jesus to give *to God the things that are God's*. We asked ourselves the question, *What belongs to God?* In this story we are told that the Macedonians *gave themselves first to the Lord*. What belongs to God? We do. What is amazing is not that we can give ourselves to the Lord but that he is willing to receive us day after day!

In this story, Paul compliments the Corinthians for their *zeal which stirred up* many Christians in Macedonia. The fact remains that the church in Corinth disappointed Paul, compelling him to practice tough love toward them. At the same time, it was with this all-too-human congregation that Paul shares one of the most eloquent and beautiful chapters about love to be found in the New Testament.

Why is God willing to receive us when we offer our lives to him? Steadfast love. Amazing grace. After Jesus called a tax collector to become a disciple and had dinner with him and his far-less-than-respectable friends, he said, *I have come not to call the righteous but sinners.*

When, day by day, we give ourselves to God, he empowers us by his Spirit to use the gifts he has given to us in ways which honor his name. We pray to God that *we may delight in your will and walk in your ways*. It is in this spirit that we reflect on the monetary implications of giving ourselves to God.

Paul's response is straight-forward and clear. *Each of you must give as you have made up your mind, not reluctantly or under compulsion, for God loves a cheerful giver.*

RELATED NOTES AND OBSERVATIONS

I CORINTHIANS 4:1,2

GALATIANS 2:1,2,10

2 CORINTHIANS 9:2
— SEE CHAPTER # 7 —
2 CORINTHIANS 8:1-2

MATTHEW 22:21

2 CORINTHIANS 8:5.

1 CORINTHIANS 5:1-2;
11:17-34
2 CORINTHIANS 13:5-10

1 CORINTHIANS 13

JOHN 3:16-17

MATTHEW 9:9-13

EVANGELICAL LUTHERAN WORSHIP, P. 95

2 CORINTHIANS 9:7
SEE ALSO
EXODUS 35:4-9. 36:1-7

And God is able to provide you with every blessing in abundance, so that by always having enough of everything, you may share abundantly in every good work. Within the freedom of the Gospel *to give as you have made up your mind,* the Macedonians *overflowed in the wealth of generosity* as an expression of *their abundant joy.*

RELATED
NOTES AND OBSERVATIONS

2 CORINTHIANS 9:8

2 CORINTHIANS 9:7

2 CORINTHIANS 8:2

[C-21]   TAXES AND GIVING   RELATED
                                                           NOTES AND OBSERVATIONS

Personal Notes and Observations
        related to taxes and giving.

*A few questions to prompt questions of your own
         related to your faith journey.*

As a person of faith, what important differences do you see between paying taxes and giving to your church?

As a person of faith, what memories come to mind as you reflect on what giving has meant to you?

As you remember a time when giving money was more an act of obligation than an opportunity to celebrate God's great love, what memories come to mind?

===

[C-21]   TAXES AND GIVING

Congregational Notes and Observations
        related to taxes and giving.

*A few questions to prompt questions of your own
         related to your congregation's ministries.*

Has your congregation ever celebrated stewardship with a song festival?

Has your congregation ever had a stewardship celebration which had its primary focus on why we give than how much we give of our time and our money?

Has your congregation ever had a stewardship celebration which provided an opportunity for lay persons to share what their given has meant to them?

THERE ARE MANY WONDERFUL HYMNS WHICH CENTER ON OUR RESPONSE TO GOD'S GREAT LOVE.

SPECIAL CHORAL AND INSTRUMENTAL MUSIC WOULD ADD TO THESE FESTIVITIES.

A CELEBRATION LIKE THIS COULD BE HELD AT ANY TIME OF THE YEAR.

[C - 22]

COUNTING THE COST

'Take care of him, and when I come back, I will repay you whatever more you spend.'

The parable of *The Good Samaritan* was told in response to a question raised by a lawyer. He asked, *Teacher, what must I do to inherit eternal life?* On another occasion this same question was posed by a *rich young man*. In both instances Jesus began by referring them to the law. However, the law was viewed in different ways by each of these men.

For the rich young man the law is centered on the Ten Commandments. He is confident he has been able to keep these commandments faithfully but wonders if this is enough.

The lawyer is asked to define the basic meaning of the law. He replies, *You shall love the Lord your God with all your heart, and with all your soul, and with all your strength, and with all your mind; and your neighbor as yourself.* He is <u>not</u> confident that he can be faithful to what the law requires, especially as it relates to loving his neighbor. This prompts him to ask another question, *Who is my neighbor?*

Reviewing this parable from a monetary perspective may be very expensive. Restricting our purpose only to the money involved may be to lose sight, at least momentarily, of many other dimensions to this parable. We dare not blind ourselves to its great importance for the church, for society and for our own faith walk. We can only hope that this limited focus will serve to sharpen our appreciation for other facets of this parable.

Counting the cost can be done by putting ourselves in the place of that man from Samaria. We can begin with the amount we earn each day. Then we take that amount and multiply it by three. The first third we have forfeited by personally spending the rest of that day and through the night taking care of the beaten man we picked up in a ditch.

RELATED NOTES AND OBSERVATIONS

LUKE 10:35
CONTEXT: LUKE 10:25-37

LUKE 10:25

MATTHEW 19:16

THE PRIMARY AREA OF THIS LAWYER'S EXPERTISE WAS IN RELIGIOUS LAW.

LUKE 10:27

LUKE 10:29

THIS PARABLE IS TOLD ONLY IN LUKE. THREE OTHER PARABLES WHICH ARE FOUND ONLY IN LUKE WERE A PART OF EARLIER CHAPTERS. THEY ARE:
"THE RICH FOOL"
— CHAPTER #8 —
" THE ELDER BROTHER"
— CHAPTER #6 —
"THE DISHONEST MANAGER"
— CHAPTER #9 —

A DENARIUS WAS THE USUAL DAY'S WAGE FOR A LABORER.

LUKE 10:34, 35

The other two-thirds of this amount is given to the innkeeper. This is an open-ended arrangement in which the Good Samaritan promises to make a further contribution if it is needed. The risk is compounded by some unknown factors. Did he have a factual basis for trusting the innkeeper? If the injuries suffered were made worse by the efforts of these well-intentioned amateurs, would they be held liable?

Counting the cost may also involve hidden costs. It is apparent that the Samaritan's time was precious to him. He could not spend more time with the injured man. It was cheaper for him to pay the innkeeper. What was the total amount of time and money he would contribute before the man who was *half dead* was able again to resume his life?

Counting the cost would not be complete if we failed to consider the possible benefits which the Samaritan may have enjoyed as the result of his good deed. If personal rewards were his motive, he may have been deeply disappointed. Only two other persons had knowledge of his compassionate generosity: the injured man and the innkeeper. The hostility between Samaritans and Jews may have prompted both of them to remain silent.

Counting the cost also depends on who is doing the counting. If the man near death in the ditch counts the cost, he would consider the time and money involved as incidental. His life was saved! He may not have headlined the fact that his life was saved by a Samaritan but his hostile attitude toward these neighbors would be challenged.

If the innkeeper counted the cost it may have made little difference whether he was a Jew or a Samaritan. The cost would not be of great concern for him. He witnessed an amazing kindness which involved neighbors who rarely spoke to each other. Speaking about it may have been hazardous for his business but it remained a beautiful memory.

As the lawyer counted the cost, he could only conclude that the lesson he had learned was very expensive. He had hoped that the Jesus would answer his question in a way that would make his religious life less demanding. Instead, the prospect of failing to achieve eternal life because he was unable to keep the law was very real. Apparently, he simply walked away to consider what he had learned.

RELATED NOTES AND OBSERVATIONS

LUKE 10:35

LUKE 10:30

How do we count the cost? Perhaps we will begin by recalling times when we had an opportunity to be a good Samaritan. However, we considered the cost to be too high. Our reactions were comparable to those of the priest and the Levite. Those memories remain painful. Is this the end of the story for us?

Again, how do we count the cost? We can turn our attention to the first question asked by the lawyer by putting ourselves in his place. We ask Jesus, *Teacher, what must I do to inherit eternal life?*

We hear him say to us, *What is written in the law?* We give the same answer as did the lawyer about loving God and loving our neighbor. Jesus says to us, *You have given the right answer; do this and you will live.*

At this point, we would not try to justify ourselves by having Jesus define who our neighbor is. We have the enormous advantage of knowing Jesus as our Savior. We live in the wake of the resurrection. Jesus promised, *Where two or three are gathered in my name, I am there among them.*

We know that Jesus fulfilled the law perfectly for us. He calls us to follow him. He gives to us the gift of faith, the gift of forgiveness, and the gift of his grace. As we reflect of the story of the Good Samaritan in terms of the gospel rather than the law, we discover many other perspectives from which we can explore its great riches.

Now we are exploring this parable only from a monetary point of view. We examine the relationship of our faith to our courage to risk a lot of money in ways which are critical for someone else but of little or no benefit to us. Our action is motivated by mercy and justice. We grasp on opportunity to do what we decide to do simply because we know it is the right thing to do.

Obviously, in this 21st century we will not do what the Good Samaritan did in this 1st century parable. If we were traveling down a road and saw a badly injured person in the ditch, we would call 911. We would stay to comfort the injured person. When an ambulance arrived, we could go on our way. Neither courage nor cash was required.

RELATED NOTES AND OBSERVATIONS

LUKE 10:25

LUKE 10:27, 28

MATTHEW 18:20

You may remember a time when you had the courage to do the right thing, not counting the cost. Now as you look back, you may not remember how much money was involved but you are not sure you would do it again. There were so many things which could have gone wrong. If this had been a historical event rather than a parable, we may have wondered if the Good Samaritan would really do it again.

A little known historical event may prompt you to remember other Good Samaritan stories. We go back to *three days in August 1991 when the Soviet Union simply disintegrated.*

First came fear. Tanks rolled into Moscow on August 19, 1991. . . . Yeltsin brought legitimacy to the new democracy . . . Key initial defenders of the Yeltsin White House came there directly from a liturgy in the Cathedral of the Assumption . . . Older women church-goers were among their supporters. *Orthodox priests ministered to some in the ring of defenders as they awaited an attack; and, after the coup collapsed, everyone used one simple word to describe it all — a miracle.*

A key event in this *miracle* took placed on August 20th. *Everyone was then expecting a military attack on the Russian White House. Young tank troops were awaiting an order from the coup leaders to crash through the ring of young people defending the fledging democratic government inside. But it was the older women who went on the attack. They moved out to scold the crew-cut troops for even thinking of attacking their pony-tailed brothers at the barricade.*

The young soldiers, lacking written commands from their superiors, were taking orders from their mothers, grandmothers, aunts, and the selfless babushkas who had brought them up and kept alive memories of Russia as a motherland. The fearsome Red Army seemed to dissolve into a band of nineteen-year-olds being cautioned against misbehavior. The older women of Russia had become for a moment "world historical figures" in a way that the Russian intelligentsia had never expected — and that Western historians have not yet recognized.

RELATED NOTES AND OBSERVATIONS

RUSSIA IN SEARCH OF ITSELF,
BY JAMES H. BILLINGTON
P. 42

P. 44

P. 45

P. 120

P. 120-121

Those good Samaritans had great courage. Cash was not a critical factor but their very lives were at risk They grasped the opportunity to do something dangerous simply because it was the right thing to do.

RELATED
NOTES AND OBSERVATIONS

[C-22] COUNTING THE COST   RELATED
                                                                   NOTES AND OBSERVATIONS

Personal Notes and Observations
   reflecting on the risks involved in compassion.

*A few questions to prompt questions of your own
   related to your faith journey.*

What are the key factors you consider as you count the cost of your giving?

What are some of the risks involved in compassionate giving in response to an urgent need?

As a thoughtful person, what are some key factors which serious givers should consider as they prepare their giving plan for the coming year or years?

===

[C-22] COUNTING THE COST

Congregational Notes and Observations related to
   compassionate giving to meet an urgent need.

*A few questions to prompt questions of your own
   related to your congregation's ministries.*

Does the parable of the Good Samaritan contain some key factors which a congregation may want to include in your vision for mission?

Is there a contingence fund in your budget which will allow the congregation to respond to immediate needs like that of a man who had been beaten and left a ditch?   LUKE 10:30

Do you have some observations you will want to share with your group about this issue?

[C-23]

MONEY AND THE LOST SON

The younger son gathered all that he had and traveled to a distant country, and there he squandered his property in dissolute living.

RELATED NOTES AND OBSERVATIONS

LUKE 15:13
CONTEXT: LUKE 15:11-32
THIS PARABLE IS FOUND ONLY IN THE GOSPEL OF LUKE.

This parable from the 1st century is of extraordinary importance for the 21st century.

It is also extraordinary for it tells two stories and consequently shares two basic truths. The first story is about the younger son; the basic truth is about redemption. The second story is about the elder brother; the basic truth is about reconciliation.

LUKE 15:11-24

LUKE 15:25-32
— CHAPTER 6 —

In this chapter we will focus on the story of the younger son and what it meant in the 1st century. On the basis of this parable about redemption, we will extend this story into the 21st century.

In the 1st century and for many centuries to follow, the elder son had first claim on the property of his father. When younger sons left home to make a new life for themselves, if they were fortunate they received financial assistance from their father.

One wonders if Joseph, Jesus' earthly father, was a younger son in his parental home. In any event, he left the area of his ancestors in Judea near the city Bethlehem to go to Galilee where jobs were available. Four miles from Nazareth the city of Sepphoris was being built by Herod Antipas. It would became the capital of Galilee. Jobs were created for construction workers which could last for a lifetime.

ARCHEOLOGISTS ARE CURRENTLY AT WORK TO REVEAL THIS ANCIENT CITY.

SEPPHORIS IS MENTIONED BY PAUL l. MAIER, A PROFESSOR OF ANCIENT HISTORY, IN THE PROLOGUE OF HIS NOVEL, *MORE THAN A SKELETON.*

This parable would immediately touch the hearts and lives of people in the 1st century. A number of their relatives had traveled to a distant land to find a new life. Generations of Jews lived out their lives in cities like Athens, Alexandria, Ephesus, Macedonia and Rome.

This parable does not name the *distant country* to which the younger son journeyed. Nor does it tell us what kind of *property* he had received from his father and had taken with him. In this 1st century parable, these are incidental details which need not be of concern as we look forward to the basic truth to be revealed.

Dissolute living is translated in various ways in other translations: *loose living, riotous living,* or a *life of debauchery.* The prodigal son ended up in a pig pen, so hungry he could have eaten the food he fed the pigs.

REVISED STANDARD VERSION, KING JAMES VERSION, JERUSALEM BIBLE.

During that humiliating experience, *he came to himself* and decided to go home. He was prepared to confess his sins before his heavenly Father and to humble himself before his father.

LUKE 15:18-19

Redemption is the basic truth of this parable. His waiting father was not concerned with the property which had been squandered. He had no intention of making a servant out of his son. With great joy he announced, *"this son of mine was dead and is alive again; he was lost and is found." And they began to celebrate.*

LUKE 15:24

There are two brief parables which introduced this parable. They can provide a bridge as we extend this 1st century parable into this 21st century.

The first parable is about a shepherd who had 100 sheep. One sheep is lost, so he leaves the 99 and goes looking for the one. Finding his property is cause for a celebration.

LUKE 15:3-6

The second parable is about a woman who has 10 silver coins. If she loses one she searches carefully until it is found. Finding her money is cause for a celebration with her friends and neighbors.

LUKE 15:8-9

The point of both parables is stated in this way:
    I tell you, there is joy in the presence of the
    angels of God over one sinner who repents.
This basic truth is of PRIMARY importance. It is also true that these brief parables affirm the secondary IMPORTANCE of property and money. Both are worth celebrating.

LUKE 15:10

RELATED NOTES AND OBSERVATIONS

As we extend the story of The Prodigal Son from the 1st century into this 21st century, we affirm the secondary IMPORTANCE of money and property without for a moment neglecting the PRIMARY importance of redemption and reconciliation. This is our story about *Money and the Lost Son*.

Those people in the 1st century believed the earth was flat and their world was around the Mediterranean Sea. In the 21st century we know the earth is round, and that our world, especially in terms of communication and commerce, is flat. There is virtually no *distant country* where a cell phone or/and e-mail cannot reach and credit cards cannot be used.

Like the Greek denarius in the Roman Empire, the America dollar is of value almost everywhere on this planet. Greek was the common language in the world of the 1st century. English is the language of commerce and diplomacy in our world today.

When our sons and daughters leave home, wherever they may go, if they have some cash and a few credit cards, *dissolute living* is offered to them. The prospect of ending up in the 21st century equivalent of a pig pen is also a sad possibility.

Parents recognize that riotous living is not the only way to ruin. Credit cards open the door for our children to live beyond their income which, unfortunately, is commonplace among adults in our country. Living on the brink of bankruptcy day after day is not what we covet for our children when they have left home to make a life for themselves.

At the least, living beyond their income results in money and/or property that is lost through exorbitant interest rates created by the abuse of credit cards. Learning to live within their income so that their money and/or property is not lost is also a cause for celebration.

It is in our interest and theirs to help our children to learn how to handle their money. It is in our interest and theirs to convince our children that credit cards are not an additional source of income. It is in our interest and theirs to teach our children that instant gratification is not the highest good.

RELATED NOTES AND OBSERVATIONS

THE WORLD IS FLAT— A BRIEF HISTORY OF THE 21ST CENTURY
THOMAS L. FRIEDMAN

"AMERICA IN THE EARLY YEARS OF THIS 21ST CENTURY CAN FAIRLY MAKE THIS STUPENDOUS CLAIM: NEVER BEFORE IN HUMAN HISTORY, INCLUDING ANY PREVIOUS ERA IN AMERICAN HISTORY, HAS A WAY OF LIFE GIVEN SO MANY PEOPLE SO MANY RICH OPPORTUNITIES TO LIVE HEALTHY, CHALLENGING, AND FULFILLING LIVES. YET THIS CLAIM INVITES THIS SHARP REBUKE: THOSE OPPORTUNITIES ARE FAR TOO OFTEN WASTED."
THE AGE OF ABUNDANCE, BRINK LINDSEY, P. 325

THE NEWLY COINED WORD "AFFLUENZA" BRINGS TO MIND THE TRAGEDIES WHICH OCCUR WHEN AFFLUENCY IS NOT APPROPRIATELY CONTROLLED.

CHILDREN LEARN FROM THEIR PARENTS.
"AMERICANS CARRIED AN AVERAGE CREDIT CARD BALANCE OF $8,400 PER HOUSEHOLD IN 2002. USING AN AVERAGE INTEREST RATE OF 15 PERCENT, THE TYPICAL U.S. FAMILY SPENDS MORE THAN $1,000 A YEAR TO AVOID PAYING CASH."
PRODIGAL SONS AND MATERIAL GIRLS.
NATHAN DUNGAN, P. 116

Yet, you may agree that an almost overwhelming silence exists within our homes and our schools and our congregations concerning these issues. Discovering ways to break that silence is a first step toward helping our children.

If you agree that your sons and daughters need to be involved in this educational and experiential opportunity, now is a good time to hear what they have to say.

If you agree that your congregation can be of significant service to your children by extending your congregation's ministries into this arena, share your thoughts with your pastor and other parents.

An approach to this serious concern may be for the stewardship board to welcome parents to a series of meetings. Parents with children in elementary school will be invited to one meeting. Parents with children in high school will attend another meeting. Parents with students in college or other institutions for advanced training would gather at another meeting.

Within a few months, the stewardship board may invite parents to another series of meetings. It may be helpful at these meetings to have the parents seated around tables. This will provide an opportunity to encourage each other and to raise questions created by this new experience with their children. The groups may want to share with the whole gathering some of the comments or questions they have been considering.

As this new ministry within the congregation becomes established, the stewardship board may want to review a decision made years ago. It was decided that only adults would receive offering envelopes, saving the cost of giving those envelopes to younger people. Perhaps special envelopes could be ordered and made available to parents involved in teaching their children about the Sharing-Saving-Spending plan.

In that wonderful 1st century parable, when the younger son who was lost comes to himself and returned home, the waiting father received him with joy.

RELATED NOTES AND OBSERVATIONS

IBID. P. 85
"ADVERTISING IS A MASSIVE, MULTIBILLION DOLLAR PROJECT THAT'S HAVING AN ENORMOUS IMPACT ON CHILD DEVELOPMENT. THANKS TO ADVERTISING, CHILDREN HAVE BECOME CONVINCED THAT THEY ARE INFERIOR IF THEY DON'T HAVE AN ENDLESS ARRAY OF NEW PRODUCTS."

IBID. P. 130
"YOUR KIDS WILL LISTEN! SEVENTY-FIVE PERCENT OF AMERICAN CHILDREN SAY THEY HAVE LEARNED THE MOST ABOUT HOW TO MANAGE MONEY FROM THEIR PARENTS."

THIS BOARD WILL CHAIR THESE MEETIINGS AND SELECT THE PERSON OR PERSONS TO SPEAK AND TO RESPOND TO QUESTIONS.

THE BOOK, *PRODIGAL SONS AND MATERIAL GIRLS*, CONTAINS SPECIFIC METHODS AS TO HOW PARENTS CAN HELP THEIR CHILDREN TO MAKE GOOD DECISIONS ABOUT THEIR MONEY.

This remains true in this 21st century. When our sons and daughters come home with affluenza, they are welcomed with open arms. Yet, how much better it would be if their parents and their congregation had prepared them to avoid affluenza in this affluent era.

The stewardship board may want to propose a special worship service reflecting this new ministry. It could be held at a time and date when seniors in high school and students in college or other institutions of advanced training could attend. These young people together with their parents would participate in this celebration.

This worship service may provide an opportunity to share some of the teachings of Jesus about money. It may involve a parent, a son or a daughter
- to read the Scripture lessons;
- to share a witness as to what the Share-Save-Spend plan has meant to them;
- to provide some special music;
- and, perhaps, to assist in the communion service.

When sharing becomes a joy rather than an obligation for these young people, they have made a discovery which will shape their lives. When saving is a way to affirming that money is their servant, not their master, they can live with a new freedom. Spending becomes a pleasure, when they know that their self-worth is not measured by how much stuff they can accumulate.

Knowing that your congregation is actively involved in helping its members to live out their Christian values by the way they handle their money is cause for a celebration.

RELATED NOTES AND OBSERVATIONS

ELCA SYNODS HAVE A STEWARDSHIP PERSON ON THEIR STAFF. IF YOU HAVE QUESTIONS OR COMMENTS CONCERNING THIS NEW MINISTRY, THIS PERSON WILL BE GLAD TO HEAR FROM YOU.

[C-23]   MONEY AND THE LOST SON   RELATED
                                                     NOTES AND OBSERVATIONS

Personal Notes and Observations reflecting our modern
    view related to money and the lost son.

*A few questions to prompt questions of your own
    related to your faith journey.*

In your family, have you tried to protect your children by keeping silent about your money?

If you give them an allowance do you expect them to keep silent as to how they spend it?

Would you be interested to guiding your children to consider the Share-Save-Spend plan?

Aware of the financial hazards which grown children often face when they leave home, do you think that your congregation can assist you and other parents with a new ministry to confront this problem?

WHAT OTHER QUESTIONS
NEED TO BE
ASKED AND ANSWERED?

===

[C-23]   MONEY AND THE LOST SON

Congregational Notes and Observations involving older
    children and their parents to provide guidance with
    reference to budgets, credit cards and cash.

*A few questions to prompt questions of your own
    related to your congregation's ministries.*

Is it appropriate for your congregation to develop a special ministry to assist parents as they guide their children in how to handle their money?

Is it appropriate for this new ministry to help young adults to avoid the hazards confronting them if they use their cash, credit cards and cell phones irresponsibly?

IS THIS A SPECIAL MINISTRY
WHICH CAN USE HELP
FROM PERSONS OUTSIDE
THE CONGREGATION?

Is it appropriate for this new ministry to provide guidance with reference to budgeting, beginning with sharing and saving and then spending?

PERHAPS AN INITIAL STEP
IN CONSIDERING THIS
NEW MINISTRY TO
TO SEEK GUIDANCE FROM
SYNOD STAFF MEMBERS.

[C-24]

RICH MAN, POOR MAN

RELATED
NOTES AND OBSERVATIONS

*There was a rich man . . . And at his gate lay
a poor man named Lazarus, covered with sores . . .*

LUKE 16:19, 20
CONTEXT: LUKE 16:19-31

Some of the details in this parable were considered in earlier chapters. The poor have a special place in the teachings of Jesus. Wealth, of itself, is not evil. Riches are to be used creatively for the greater good.

THIS PARABLE IS FOUND
ONLY IN LUKE.

In this parable the rich man's name is unknown. One day our Lord was confronted by another rich man who was not named. There are a number of persons blessed with wealth who are named, including some women who supported Jesus and his disciples *out of their resources,* including Salome the mother of James and John.

LUKE 8:1-3
MARK 15:40-41

The disciples of Jesus did not consider themselves to be poor. Four of them were fishermen who left their business behind to follow Christ. Matthew was a tax collector who left behind his wealth producing occupation as he followed Jesus. In the writings of St. Paul we are assured that we need not be conquered by poverty nor corrupted by wealth.

MATTHEW 19:23-26

2 CORINTHIANS 8:9-14

The primary point of this parable has its focus on two closely related topics which we have not considered in previous chapters.

We begin with Lazarus. More important than his poverty, Lazarus is known for his piety. His name means *he whom God hears.* The rich man knew this poor man for he knew his name. It is also apparent that Lazarus knew him and his family for the rich man wanted Lazarus to warn his brothers.

THIS LAZARUS IS,
OF COURSE, A PERSON IN
A PARABLE. THE OTHER
LAZARUS NAMED IN
JOHN 11:1-44
IS THE BROTHER OF
MARY AND MARTHA.

LUKE 16:24, 27

The rich man was *dressed in purple and fine linen.* Purple was a rich cloth dyed with the liquid obtained from a species of shellfish. Obviously, it was very expensive.

LUKE 16:19
ANNOTATION IN THE
*OXFORD ANNOTATED
BIBLE,* P. 108NT

122

The vast extent of the rich man's wealth is also indicated by the fact that he *feasted sumptuously every day*. This daily extravagance makes it clear that his wealth went far beyond the riches which the disciples left behind and the wealth of the women who used their resources to support the ministry of Jesus.

While the rich man was feasting with his friends, Lazarus *longed to satisfy his hunger with what fell from the rich man's table; even the dogs would come to lick his sores.* We are told that among the super-rich in that ancient time, bread could serve as a napkin. A piece of bread was used to wipe off remnants of foods and fluids around the mouth. It would then be thrown on the floor to be devoured by the dogs.

This is in stark contrast to the teachings of Jesus. He said, *When you give a banquet, invite the poor, the crippled, the lame, and the blind. And you will be blessed, because they cannot repay you, for you will be repaid at the resurrection of the righteous.*

Surrounding the topics we want to consider is imagery concerning *Abraham's bosom* and *hades*. The imagery used in parables is not to be taken literally. The reality of heaven and hell is clearly taught in the Bible but this imagery only serves to capture our attention.

Abraham's bosom is translated *with Abraham* and *Lazarus by his side.* Abraham is the father of the faithful. He is God's friend. This imagery suggests that Lazarus is in heaven. *Hades* is a translation of words like *sheol* and *gehenna*. *Sheol* speaks of the underworld, the realm of the dead. *Gehenna* brings to mind the garbage dump near Jerusalem where fire was an on-going necessity. The rich man dies, is buried, and discovers that he has gone to a very unpleasant place.

Reflecting on this parable from a monetary perspective opens the door to the two topics which merit our attention. First, how we use our wealth in this life serves as a measure of our faith. Among Jews and the early Christians taking care of the poor was a basic first step toward righteous living.

RELATED NOTES AND OBSERVATIONS

LUKE 16:19

LUKE 16:21

LUKE 14:13, 14

ABRAHAM'S BOSOM IS IMAGERY USED IN THE KING JAMES' VERSION OF THE BIBLE.

THE BOOK *THE GREAT DIVORCE* BY C. S. LEWIS ALSO USES IMAGERY TO CAPTURE OUR ATTENTION REGARDING HEAVEN AND HELL.

LUKE 16:22, 23

LUKE 16:23-31

A THEOLOGICAL WORD BOOK OF THE BIBLE, P. 106-107

LUKE 16:23-26

ACTS 4:32-35

Second, this parable underscores for all of us that if we do not heed the witness of the law and the prophets, we will remain unconvinced even if a faithful friend arises from the dead to provide a further witness. As Christians, we have the witness of the risen Christ.

As we reflect on this parable in terms of our own time, two possibilities confront us. We may begin by making a comparison between rich man, poor man in our country. The yearly income of a rich man is currently almost beyond belief greater than for a poor man. Our own wealth may appear to be singularly unimpressive.

The second possibility is to measure our own wealth against the history of other persons on our small planet. *Men and women at middle-class standards or above in the U.S. now live better than 99.4% of the human beings who have ever existed.*

We can also measure our wealth against that of the poor in our country. *Working a 40 hour week at the current federal minimum wage, taking no time off, translates to less than $11,000 a year. The current Department of Labor poverty line for a family of four is $18,100 per annum.*

We can also measure our wealth against the poor on our planet. *One point two billion people in the world live on $1.08 or less a day. A billion people in the world . . . pay a quarter of their daily income for small amounts of clean water.* Against this background our own wealth is very impressive indeed.

As we give our attention to Lazarus in this parable another possibility arises. In the parable the rich man and Lazarus knew each other. Perhaps at one time Lazarus was also very rich. Then he was struck down by a catastrophic disease which not only robbed him of his health but also of his wealth. Wealthy folks like us know that this is an ever present possibility.

Catastrophic disease is only one scenario which can destroy wealth. Within a few moments of reflection we can call to mind many other possibilities which would leave us in poverty.

RELATED NOTES AND OBSERVATIONS

LUKE 16:31

JOHN 20:24-29

IN 1948 NOBEL LAUREATE PAUL SAMUELSON ATTEMPTED TO ILLUSTRATE THE DIFFERENCE IN INCOME BETWEEN THE RICHEST MEN AND OTHER AMERICANS BY USING A CHILD'S BUILDING BLOCKS.

EACH LAYER OF BLOCKS EQUALS $1,000 OF YEARLY INCOME. TO REACH THE INCOME OF THE VERY RICH THIS PYRAMID WOULD GO HIGHER THAN THE EIFFEL TOWER. THE INCOME OF MOST AMERICANS WOULD BE MEAURED WITHIN A YARD FROM THE GROUND, . *ECONOMICS: AN INTRODUCTORY ANALYSIS*, P. A. SAMUELSON, P. 63.

THE PROGRESS PARADOX. GLENN EASTERBOOK, P. 80

IBID, P. 260

IBID, P. 282

SEE ALSO *NICKEL AND DIMED* BARBARA EHRENREICH

IN 1998, SAMUELSON FOUND THAT THE EIFFEL TOWER WAS NO LONGER AN ADQUATE COMPARISON. HE REPLACED IT WITH MOUNT EVEREST. *ECONOMICS*, P.A. SAMUELSON AND WM. NORDHAUS, P. 359.

It is also true that a person experiencing poverty can become exceedingly wealthy. Further, one person can go from poverty to wealth, back to poverty and then forward to another fortune during the course of a lifetime. Both poverty and wealth are transient. And so are we.

The decisions we make in our lives will have consequences beyond this life. Poverty can create cynicism. Wealth can create arrogance. Cynicism and arrogance may view God as irrelevant. Beyond this life it is too late to repent for the way we have lived.

Rich man, poor man, every person has the opportunity to live and to die enfolded by the grace of God. This is not an achievement earned through poverty nor paid for by wealth. It is always a gift from God.

In this parable the rich man needed the poor man. The piety of Lazarus could provide an example of how eternal wealth can be found. In this parable, Lazarus needed the rich man. He had the right to expect the rich man to provide from his abundance the food he needed to keep from starving to death. Lazarus, *he whom God hears*, could then offer prayers of thanksgiving to God for the compassionate piety of his rich friend.

In our 21st century, this kind of personal contact between the rich and the poor is a very rare experience. Our ongoing support for church agencies and other charitable organizations is a way for us to reach out with food for the poor. This way does not reflect righteous living if the amount we give does not reflect our compassion for the poor.

In our 21st century, some rich persons are sharing their wealth with millions of ambitious persons enabling them to break out of the dead-end cycles of poverty. Loans as small as $35 create enterprises that mean food, clothing and dignity for the poorest of the poor around the world.

RELATED NOTES AND OBSERVATIONS

EPHESIANS 2:4-10

MATTHEW 6:19-21

THE MIRACLES OF BAREFOOT CAPITALISM
BY JIM KLOBUCHAR AND SUSAN CORNELL WILKES

[C-24]   RICH MAN, POOR MAN   RELATED
                                                   NOTES AND OBSERVATIONS

Personal Notes and Observations
      concerning rich folks and poor folks.

   *A few questions to prompt questions of your own
          related to your faith journey.*

   As a person of wealth will your faith journey be enriched if your daily devotions include prayers for the poor?

   As a person experiencing poverty, will your faith journey be enriched if your daily devotions include prayers for the rich?

   How does your prayer life impact the economic realities with which poor folks and rich folks live day after day?

THE PARABLE UNDER
CONSIDERATION IS ABOUT
MEN.
PLEASE ALLOW THE WORD
MAN TO INCLUDE BOTH
MEN AND WOMEN.

===

[C-24]   RICH MAN, POOR MAN

Congregational Notes and Observations
      concerning rich folks and poor folks.

   *A few questions to prompt questions of your own
          related to your congregation's ministries.*

   As a congregation you pray for the poor. How do your actions reflect your prayers in behalf of the poor?

   Has your congregation ever faced poverty? What did you learn from this experience?

   Has your congregation ever faced wealth? What did you learn from this experience?

[C-25]

PHARISEE / TAX COLLECTOR / TITHING

RELATED NOTES AND OBSERVATIONS

He told this parable to some who trusted in themselves that they were righteous and regarded others with contempt: . . .

LUKE 18:9
CONTEXT: LUKE 18:9-14

TITHING - LUKE 11:42, MATTHEW 23:23

THIS PARABLE IS FOUND ONLY IN LUKE.

Jesus was a great story-teller. Occasionally in his parables, he used humor to capture the attention of the listeners. At other times, he used hyperbole to make the point of the parable abundantly clear.

In this parable hyperbole is used to describe clearly who is the good guy and who is the bad guy. The bad guy was absolutely confident that he was the good guy. The good guy saw himself as the bad guy who pleaded for mercy.

The point of this parable is revealed in the opening verse of this text and centers around the word *contempt*. The Pharisee regarded with contempt *thieves, rogues, adulterers* and that *tax collector*.

LUKE 18:9

LUKE 18:11

The Pharisee saw himself as righteous for *he was not like other people*. He proclaimed, *I fast twice a week, I give a tenth of all my income*. In this story fasting and tithing are simply ornaments on a cloak of self-righteousness.
`

LUKE 18:12

Under religious law, fasting was practiced only on special occasions like the Day of Atonement. He fasted every Monday and Thursday. In the 1st century among Pharisees the tithe pertained specifically to *mint, dill, and cummin,* or, in Luke, to *mint and rue and herbs of all kinds*. This Pharisee gave a tithe *of all my income*.

CUMMIN — A PLANT OF THE CARROT FAMILY CULTIVATED FOR ITS AROMATIC SEEDS WHICH WERE USED AS A SPICE.
MATTHEW 23:23
LUKE 11:42
LUKE 18:12
RUE— A MEDICINAL HERB.

These noteworthy disciplines of piety become shameful when they are motivated by self-righteousness. They become outrageous when they are used to show contempt for a sinner who is pleading for mercy before God.

LUKE 18:13

Our Lord makes it clear that the tax collector *went down to his home justified.* The proud Pharisee *will be humbled.* As we ponder this conclusion it is apparent that we must not show contempt for either person.

We remember that Saul, like his father before him, had been a Pharisee. His zeal as a Pharisee prompted him to become a persecutor of the followers of Christ. He became Paul whose zeal as a Christian prompted him to bring the Gospel to the Gentiles, to us.

We also remember Levi, who was a tax collector. He became Matthew, a disciple of our Lord. As we read the New Testament, we begin with The Gospel According to Matthew.

As we review the Gospels from a monetary perspective, this parable provides a marvelous opportunity to consider tithing within the framework of the Gospel.

Our Lord makes it clear that giving a tenth of our income is be practiced provided we have *not neglected the weightier matters of the law: justice and mercy and faith.* In Luke the wording is a bit different. Tithing is to be practiced without neglecting *justice and the love of God.*

Our Lord gave us a Gospel guideline for giving in the Sermon on the Mount. He said, *When you give alms, do not let your left hand know what your right hand is doing, so that your alms may be done in secret; and your Father who sees in secret will reward you.*

That this is a guideline and not a new law is indicated when Jesus was watching as people brought their gifts to the temple. *He saw a poor widow put in two small copper coins. He said, 'Truly I tell you, this poor widow has put in more than all of them; for all of them have contributed out of their abundance, but she out of her poverty has put in all she had to live on.'* Her gift, reflecting her *love of God* would not remain a secret.

However, the guideline remains. Most of the time tithing is practiced quietly. Sometimes, so quietly that other folks are stunned when they become aware of the tithers in their midst.

RELATED NOTES AND OBSERVATIONS
LUKE 18:14

ACTS 23:6
ACTS 9:1-19

LUKE 5:27-28

MATTHEW 23:23

LUKE 11:42

MATTHEW 6:3,4

LUKE 21:1-4

These persons would be amazed to discover that there are other givers who give 20% of their income. Some, like Zacchaeus, give at the 50% level. A few persons give at a higher level. They do not reflect the pride and arrogance of the Pharisee in this parable.

In Gospel giving, it is also true that the tithe is not the lower limit for giving as a Christian. Some parents have several of their children in college at the same time. They suffer what has been called *maltuition*. For a time their giving drops below the tithe until their lives return to normal. Similar difficult times for other givers produce similar results.

We always remain free to raise or lower our giving without calling into question our love for God or our concern for justice.

Another factor merits our consideration. The Holy Spirit gives many gifts to Christians. Not all Christians have the same gifts. Generosity is one of the gifts of the Spirit. Persons who have received this gift are not to sit in judgment over those who are not gifted in this way.

GALATIANS 5:22,23
WHEN WE ENCOURAGE CHRISTIANS TO PRAY FOR THE GIFTS OF THE SPIRIT, IT IS IMPORTANT TO AFFIRM THE GIFT OF GENEROSITY.

An editor of a newspaper in a small mid-western town penned words years ago which remain in memory. He wrote about the four joys of money. The first joy is to earn some money. The second joy is to save some of it. The third joy is to spend some of it. The greatest joy is to give some of it away.

Many Christians would affirm those four joys as correct, but suggest they are listed a bit backward. First experience the joy of sharing, then enjoy saving some of it, and then have the fun of spending the rest of it. Of fundamental importance is to give thanks to God for giving us the strength and skill and opportunity to earn some of it.

2 CORINTHIANS 8:1-5

Persons who have experienced this *greatest joy* do not consider tithing as sacrificial giving. Further, the joy of generosity is experienced by persons at every income level, including the very poor and the very wealthy.

An old formula continues to make sense — 10, 10, 80. First, share 10%; second, save 10%; third, spend with thanksgiving 80% of your income.

RELATED NOTES AND OBSERVATIONS

When young adults follow that formula, they will have adopted a pattern which will serve them well. As they grow older, they may enjoy revising this formula, increasing the sharing and saving portions for they can still live with contentment on the money that remains.

The apostle Paul never used the word *tithe* in his letters to the churches. He practiced generosity in his own special way by supporting himself as a tent maker. He did not want to become a financial burden for his young congregations.

ACTS 18:1-4

Paul taught new Christians to give in proportion to their resources, and to plan ahead. He clearly informed them that their gifts were essential to provide food for the hungry in Jerusalem. And, he did not fail to thank the givers for their generosity and faithfulness to the Gospel.

I CORINTHIANS 16:1-4

PHILIPPIANS 4:15-20

Generosity begins with our gifts to the congregation to which we belong. Here our own spiritual needs are met, and our children are nurtured by the Gospel.

Generosity continues through our congregation as we reach out to serve people who are physically and spiritual hungry around and far beyond our communities. We give to strengthen our colleges and seminaries as they prepare persons for service in this country and around the world.

Generosity also involves our support for causes of special interest to us. These agencies employ persons who have skills we may not possess. We strengthen them with our financial support and with our prayers.

Above all, generosity is our response to God's gracious generosity toward each one of us.

[C-25]   PHARISEE / TAX COLLECTOR / TITHING   RELATED
                                                NOTES AND OBSERVATIONS

Personal Notes and Observations
        reflecting on the pro's and con's of tithing.

*A few questions to prompt questions of your own
        related to your faith journey.*

   If you tithe in response to the Gospel would you be willing to share with others what tithing has meant for you as a part of your faith journey?

   Have you had opportunities to listen to other persons who tithe? What did you learn from those experiences?

   As a person of faith, do you think that growing beyond the tithe becomes a measure of one's faith?

===

[C-25]   PHARISEE / TAX COLLECTOR / TITHER

Congregational Notes and Observations
        concerning the pro's and con's of tithing.

*A few questions to prompt questions of your own
        related to your congregation's ministries.*

   Does your congregation encourage its members to tithe as a Gospel opportunity?

   Is is made clear that tithing may be practiced if a person has *not neglected the weightier matters of the law: justice, mercy and faith?*

MATTHEW 23:23

   Does your congregation practice tithing its own financial resources with reference to supporting ministries around and far beyond your congregation?

TITHING DOES NOT LIMIT
THE SPENDING PLAN OF
THE CONGREGATION'S
SUPPORT FOR MISSION
TO 10%. IT MAY
BE VIEWED AS A
BEGINNING POINT.

   Does this way of thinking and planning encourage members of the congregation to give consideration to tithing for themselves?

[C-26]

SALVATION NOW!

'Today salvation has come to this house, because he too is a son of Abraham. For the Son of Man came to seek out and to save the lost.'

LUKE 19:9-10
CONTEXT: LUKE 19:1-10

The story of Zacchaeus is an up-side-down version of the parable of the Prodigal Son. Both were lost. Both of these texts deal with a lot of money. One was lost as he squandered his inherited wealth in loose living. The other was lost in the pursuit of wealth as he turned his back on his spiritual inheritance as a *son of Abraham.*

THIS EVENT IS RECORDED ONLY IN LUKE.

LUKE 19:9

Zacchaeus was a *chief tax collector* who was literally up a tree when Jesus found him. Jericho was on a main trade route, and Zacchaeus had contracted for the right to collect revenue in that district. He *was rich.* And he was despised as a traitor who gained wealth by cooperating with the Roman oppressors.

LUKE 19:2

He heard that Jesus would be passing through Jericho. He wanted to see him so he climbed that tree in order to peer over the crowd. He was in for a surprise which transformed his life.

Jesus saw him and called out, *"Zacchaeus, hurry up and come down, for I must stay at your house today."* So he hurried down and was happy to welcome him.

LUKE 19:5-6

The crowd was also surprised but they were not pleased. They grumbled and said, *"He has gone to be the guest of one who is a sinner."*

LUKE 19:7

We have noted these details carefully for both our Lord's words and the response of the crowd suggest that, at this point, there was a lapse of time. We are not told what Jesus and Zacchaeus talked about or how long they were together in his house. When they came out, the crowd was still waiting for them. The greatest surprise of all was quickly revealed.

Zacchaeus stood there and said to the Lord, "Look, half of my possessions, Lord, I will give to the poor; and if I have defrauded anyone of anything, I will pay back four times as much."

RELATED NOTES AND OBSERVATIONS

LUKE 19:8

Zacchaeus makes a vow to give to the poor an amount far exceeding a tithe. Ancient religious law required that anyone who took anything *by robbery or by fraud . . . shall repay the principal amount and shall add one-fifth to it.* Again, Zacchaeus goes far beyond that law.

LEVITICUS 6:4-5

This chief tax collector, whose life had been governed by greed, found the freedom in Christ to live a new life. From that day forward he would be guided by *the weightier matters of the law: justice, mercy, and faith.*

MATTHEW 23:23

A few days earlier Jesus was confronted by another rich man who wanted to know what he had to do to inherit eternal life. This encounter had a sad ending. Jesus told his disciples, *"It is easier for a camel to go through the eye of a needle than for someone who is rich to enter the kingdom of God."*

LUKE 18:18-27

LUKE 18:25

This encounter with Zacchaeus provides clear evidence that *what is impossible for mortals is possible for God.* It has a jubilant ending. With great joy Jesus proclaims, *"Today salvation has come to this house."*

LUKE 18:27

LUKE 19:9A

How could this happen? Did Zacchaeus find a way to use his money to gain access into the Kingdom of God. No. He gained access into the Kingdom *because he too is a son of Abraham.*

LUKE 19:9B

Like the prodigal son, Zacchaeus returned home to his father. His spiritual father and ours was Abraham, the father of the faithful. Greed had robbed Zacchaeus of his faith. Now his faith took control over his possessions.

LUKE 15:11-32

Once he was lost. Now salvation gave him new freedom, new joy, and new purpose for his life. He became a new creation in Christ: *everything old has passed away; see, everything has become new.*

LUKE 19:10

2 CORINTHIANS 5:17

His money was no longer a self-centered testimony to his professional success and power. His money was now an instrument of mercy and justice.

Is Zacchaeus a realistic example for us in this 21st century? Or, is he simply like an ancient star in the heavens; someone to be admired but whose actions are far beyond anything we can match?

What might happen to us if we climbed up a tree to catch a glimpse of Christ passing by? What if Jesus made it clear that he wanted to be a guest within our homes? Are we open to a surprising and joyful transformation in our lives?

Faith, Jesus taught us, can move mountains. Miracles of science have become common-place in our time. Can miracles of faith be far behind?

Have we overlooked something here? What we have failed to acknowledge clearly is not something but someone. This miracle of faith became possible because *the Son of Man came to seek out and to save the lost.*

Jesus *came to seek out* Zacchaeus. He wanted to be invited into Zacchaeus' home because he came *to save the lost.* It was by his power that Zacchaeus was given new life, new hope, new purpose. The miracle of faith is always a gift from God. Mission giving bears witness to this gift from our heavenly Father.

One of the hymns of the church poses a series of questions which our Lord asks, inviting our response. This poetry provides a vision for mission which, if it is not personal is not powerful.

> *"I, the Lord of sea and sky,*
>   *I have heard my people cry.*
> *All who dwell in deepest sin*
>   *my hand will save.*
> *I, who made the stars of night,*
>   *I will make their darkness bright,*
> *Who will bear my light to them,*
>   *Whom shall I send?"*

RELATED NOTES AND OBSERVATIONS

ONE OF OUR TABLE PRAYERS BEGINS *COME, LORD JESUS, BE OUR GUEST.*

MATTHEW 17:20

LUKE 19:10

"I, the Lord of snow and rain,
      I have borne my people's pain.
I have wept for love of them.
      They turn away.
I will break their hearts of stone,
      give them hearts for love alone.
I will speak my word to them.
      Whom shall I send?"

"I, the Lord of wind and flame,
      I will tend the poor and lame.
I will set a feast for them,
      My hand will save.
Finest bread I will provide
      till their hearts are satisfied.
I will give my life for them,
      Whom shall I send?"

Here I am, Lord. Is it I, Lord?
      I have heard your calling in the night.
I will go, Lord, if you lead me.
      I will hold your people in my heart.

HERE I AM, LORD
HYMN # 574, TEXT AND
MUSIC BY
DANIEL SCHUTTE.
EVANGELICAL
LUTHERAN WORSHIP

[C-26] SALVATION NOW!

Personal Notes and Observations
reflecting on money and a new way of life.

A few questions to prompt questions of your own related to your faith journey.

As you reflect on your faith journey, when did you learn to think about your money in terms of world-wide mission? What impact did this have on your life?

Through your own encounter with Jesus, has your faith journey had a special mission focus for you?

Have you had an opportunity to share what you have learned about money and mission with your children? How did they react to this view of money?

===================================
[C-26] SALVATION NOW!

Congregational Notes and Observations
reflecting on money and encounters with Jesus.

A few questions to prompt questions of your own related to your congregation's ministries.

Does your congregation see money in terms of a world-wide mission?

Are there specific ways in which your congregation lives out its mission with passion and persistence?

Does your congregation enable some of its leaders to participate in its world-wide mission so they can share with members what they have experienced?

[C-27]

CONCLUDING CONTRASTS

RELATED NOTES AND OBSERVATIONS

Mary took a pound of costly perfume made of pure nard, anointed Jesus' feet, and wiped them with her hair.

JOHN 12:3
CONTEXT: JOHN 12:1-13

We began at the beginning of the Gospel According to Matthew. It was not known how many chapters would be needed to review the Gospels with reference to *Jesus' Teachings about Money*. Nor was it known what text would confront us for this concluding chapter.

As it turns out, we are confronted by contrasts. This event in the life of our Lord reveals the contrast between Mary's gift from her heart and the greed in the heart of Judas Iscariot.

THIS EVENT IS RECORDED ONLY IN JOHN'S GOSPEL.

JOHN 12:3-7

In the background is the wondrous miracle of new life for Lazarus. This is contrasted with the malice of the chief priests whose goal was to put both Jesus and Lazarus to death.

JOHN 12:9-11

The next day leads us to the greatest contrast. On Palm Sunday, crowds welcomed Jesus to Jerusalem. *Hosanna! Blessed is the one who comes in the name of the Lord — the King of Israel!*

JOHN 12:12,13

Then, on Good Friday, another crowd shouted, *Crucify him!* They were offended when a sign on his cross proclaimed, *Jesus of Nazareth, the King of the Jews.*

JOHN 19:15
JOHN 19:19

A closer look may give us clearer vision as we try to comprehend these contrasts.

We focus on Mary and Martha. As Mary anoints the feet of Jesus, we remember her earlier experience with our Lord. It was the time when she sat at Jesus' feet, listening to him. Martha complained for she needed her sister's help.

LUKE 10:38-42

137

A more recent memory centered on their brother, Lazarus. He was seriously ill, near death. They sent a message to Jesus pleading with him to come quickly.

Mary and Martha were convinced that if Jesus were there, Lazarus would not die. Four days before Jesus came, Lazarus did die and was buried. Their tears flowed as they poured out their grief to him, and he wept with them. Then Jesus raised Lazarus from the dead!

JOHN 11:1-45

Mary, Martha and Lazarus wanted to express their love for Jesus in a special way. A jar of *pure nard* was purchased. It was a costly gift but the gift of new life for Lazarus was far more precious. Further, it was a gift of a lifetime for Jesus' death was just a few days away.

IT WOULD REQUIRE THE WAGES OF A LABORER FOR ALMOST A WHOLE YEAR TO PURCHASE THIS POUND OF PERFUME.

Mary took this costly perfume, anointed Jesus feet, and wiped them with her hair. In the 1st century, it is hard to imagine a greater act of faith-filled devotion, tender love and humble gratitude.

JOHN 12:7,8
COMPARING THIS STORY WITH A SIMILAR STORY IN MARK 14:3-9 IS HIGHLY RECOMMENDED.

The contrast between Mary's act and the complaint raised by Judas makes his question almost an obscenity. *Why was this perfume not sold for three hundred denarii and the money given to the poor?*

JOHN 12:4-5

The disciples were disgusted. They knew that Judas was a thief. He did not care about the poor. He kept their common purse and would steal from it.

JOHN 12:6

Jesus did not hesitate to accept this costly gift. He treasured this final act of devotion as he prepared to offer himself on the cross for the sake of us all, including Judas.

JOHN 12:7

With patient compassion, Jesus explained to Judas that giving gifts to the poor was an ongoing opportunity. He did not embarrass Judas by revealing his hypocrisy.

JOHN 12:8

The next great contrast involves the news spreading throughout Bethany that Jesus was there. A great crowd gathered. They wanted to see Jesus; they were also interested in seeing Lazarus.

JOHN 12:9

This spontaneous gathering may be seen as an expression of faith and devotion. For some folks in that crowd, it may have been a new found faith in Christ.

The contrast here is with the chief priests who planned to put Jesus to death and now *planned to put Lazarus to death as well, since on account of him many of the Jews were deserting and were believing in Jesus.*

JOHN 12:10

The chief priests did not see themselves as evil. The logic behind their plans was voiced by the high priest, Caiaphas. He said to them concerning Jesus, *It is better to have one man die for the people than to have the whole nation perish.*

JOHN 11:34
LATER THIS LOGIC WAS CHALLENGED BY GAMALIEL, THE RENOWNED TEACHER OF SAUL/PAUL. SEE ACTS 5:33-42; 22:3.

The greatest contrast involves what happened on the following day, Palm Sunday. Within a few days, we are confronted by the history changing events of Good Friday followed by Easter Sunday.

On Palm Sunday the crowds showed their eager expectation as they welcomed Jesus as the *King of Israel.* In the wake of Easter, we know him as the *King of kings and Lord of lords.*

JOHN 12:12-13

JOHN 12:13

REVELATION 19:16

This closer look allows us to see these events from the 1st century as a portrayal in miniature of events which surround us in this 21st century.

We are surprised with joy as we discover grace filled moments involving thanksgiving, generosity, love, and devotion. Many of these special occasions in our day, like that of Mary in this story, are private affairs which shun praise and publicity.

We may compare these current events with the widow and her two pennies, with Joseph of Arimathea and Nicodemus bringing gifts of myrrh, aloes and spices at the burial of Jesus, or with the Wise Men who brought gifts of gold, frankincense, and myrrh to the Christ child.

These events from the 1st century may bring to mind persons or groups in this 21st century for whom money is of SECONDARY importance.

The list of events which come to your mind will be your own. Other lists from other persons will also be very personal. These lists will be like a warm, powerful light which can dispel the cold darkness.

We are sadly accustomed to learn of disgraceful acts by leaders to be found in every field of endeavor. As was true in the 1st century, these leaders in our day find ways to justify their cruel behavior.

As we look within our own lives, we may wonder what we can do as a special, once in a lifetime act of devotion, through which we express thanksgiving and love for our Lord. We are not looking for praise or publicity.

Our motivation is similar to that of Lazarus and his sisters. We have been given a new life. Our new life became possible through our Lord's sacrificial death. Our new life begins now and continues on forever in the presence of our risen Lord.

With thanks to God we offer our closing prayer even as the music of this familiar hymn echoes in our mind.

Beautiful Savior, King of creation,
Son of God and Son of Man!
Truly I'd love thee, Truly I'd serve thee,
Light of my soul, my joy, my crown.

Fair are the meadows, Fair are the woodlands,
Robed in flowers of blooming spring;
Jesus is fairer, Jesus is purer,
He makes our sorrowing spirit sing.

Beautiful Savior, Lord of the nations,
Son of God and Son of Man!
Glory and honor, Praise, adoration,
Now and forevermore be thine!

Amen.

RELATED NOTES AND OBSERVATIONS

2 CORINTHIANS 5:17-21

ROMANS 6:5-12

REVELATION 21:1-5

BEAUTIFUL SAVIOR, HYMN # 838, EVANGELICAL LUTHERAN WORSHIP

[M-27]   CONCLUDING   CONTRASTS   RELATED
                                                 NOTES AND OBSERVATIONS

Personal Notes and Observations
        reflecting on extraordinary gifts.

  *A few questions to prompt questions of your own
          related to your faith journey.*

Have you come to a point in your faith journey when you are considering offering an extraordinary gift to your congregation or to a special mission endeavor which has touched your life?

Have you shared your thoughts with your spouse or with your family or with your pastor? Have specific plans been formulated to give substance to your vision?

You may be confronted by persons who don't approve of your extraordinary gift. Does this concern you?

===

[M-27]   CONCLUDING   CONTRASTS

Congregational Notes and Observations
        pertaining to extraordinary gifts.

  *A few questions to prompt questions of your own
          related to your congregation's ministries.*

Is your congregation prepared to accept and honor extraordinary gifts?

Has a pamphlet been prepared which outlines how these gifts can be given, and specific guidelines as to how the congregation will use them?

When requested, is your congregation prepared to accept an extraordinary gift without revealing the donor?

Are there certain kinds of gifts which need prior approval before they can be received?

141

BIBLICAL REFERENCES

NEW TESTAMENT
BASIC TEXTS:
MATTHEW 2:1-23; 1, 2
MATTHEW 3:1-17; 6
MATTHEW 4:1-11; 11-13
MATTHEW 4:18-22; 15,17
MATTHEW 5:1-7:28; 20
MATTHEW 5:21-26; 25
MATTHEW 6:1-4; 30
MATTHEW 6:19-21; 35
MATTHEW 6:24; 40. 45, 46
MATTHEW 6:25-34; 52,53,57,60
MATTHEW 10:1-15; 62,63
MATTHEW 13:1-53; 67-72
MATTHEW 14:13-21; 73
MATTHEW 16:24-28; 78
MATTHEW 18:23-35; 83-85
MATTHEW 19:16-26; 70,88-93
MATTHEW 20:1-16; 95,96
MATTHEW 21:12-17; 100,101
MATHEW 22:15-22; 105,106

RELATED TEXTS:
MATTHEW 1:1-17,25; 100
MATTHEW 3:2; 6
MATTHEW 4:3-4; 75
MATTHEW 4:18-22; 90
MATTHEW 5:16; 30,31
MATTHEW 5:43-44; 106
MATTHEW 6:2-4; 7
MATTHEW 6:3-4; 128
MATTHEW 6:10; 54
MATTHEW 6:12; 86
MATTHEW 6:19-21; 125
MATTHEW 6:24; 40,46
MATTHEW 7:1; 52
MATTHEW 9:9; 90
MATTHEW 9:9-13; 107
MATTHEW 10:3; 2
MATTHEW 10:4; 90
MATTHEW 11:2-19; 6,8
MATTHEW 12:46-50; 2
MATTHEW 13:11; 60,69
MATTHEW 13:45-56; 59
MATTHEW 15:21-28; 63
MATTHEW 16:16,21; 79
MATTHEW 17:1-8; 78,80
MATTHEW 17:20; 134
MATTHEW 17:24-28; 101
MATTHEW 18:1-5; 74
MATTHEW 18:1-5; 74
MATTHEW 18:15-17; 83
MATTHEW 18:20; 112
MATTHEW 19:16-26; 88
MATTHEW 19:23-26; 91,122
MATTHEW 19:24-26; 20
MATTHEW 20:20-28; 12
MATTHEW 21:28-46; 68
MATTHEW 22:15-22; 107
MATTHEW 22:23-33; 88
MATTHEW 23:23; 128,133
MATTHEW 24:45-51; 41
MATTHEW 25:14-46; 46
MATTHEW 25:31-40; 33
MATTHEW 25:34-36; 89
MATTHEW 26:6-13; 30,89
MATTHEW 26:14-16; 42
MATTHEW 26:15; 1
MATTHEW 27:3-10; 42
MATTHEW 27:57; 38
MATTHEW 27:58-61; 2
MATTHEW 28:13-15; 42
MATTHEW 28:19; 28,63,64

BASIC TEXTS:
MARK 1:1-11; 6,17
MARK 1:12-13; 11,12
MARK 1:16-20; 15
MARK 4:1-34; 67
MARK 6:7-13; 62
MARK 6:30-44; 73,74
MARK 8:34-37; 78
MARK 10:17-31; 55,89,90
MARK 11:11, 15-19; 100
MARK 12:13-17; 108

RELATED TEXTS:
MARK 1:1-4; 6, 101
MARK 9:2-13; 79
MARK 14:3-9; 30
MARK 14:10-12; 105
MARK 15:40,41; 38,122

BASIC TEXTS:
LUKE 1:5-80; 6,101
LUKE 4:1-13; 11-13
LUKE 5:1-11; 15-17
LUKE 6:17-7:1; 20
LUKE 8:1-15; 67,88
LUKE 8:30; 122
LUKE 9:1-16; 10:1-13; 63
LUKE 9:10-17; 73
LUKE 9:23-27; 70
LUKE 10:25-37; 110-115,114
LUKE 12:22-34; 52,57
LUKE 12:42-44; 59
LUKE 15:11-32; 116,117
LUKE 16:19-31; 122-124
LUKE 18:9-14; 127-128
LUKE 18:18-30; 88
LUKE 19:1-10; 132-134
LUKE 19:45-48; 100
LUKE 20:20-26; 105

RELATED TEXTS:
LUKE 1:5-2:20; 101
LUKE 2:41-51; 101
LUKE 3:1-22; 6,10
LUKE 3:23-38; 101
LUKE 4:38-39; 18
LUKE 5:27-28; 128
LUKE 7:18-29.16:16; 8
LUKE 8:1-3; 38,122
LUKE 10:1-12; 62
LUKE 10:13-20; 63
LUKE 10:38-42; 137
LUKE 11:42; 128
LUKE 12:1; 36
LUKE 12:13-21; 35,36,52
LUKE 12:22-34; 52,54,55
LUKE 14:13,14; 123
LUKE 15:1-7; 63
LUKE 15:11-32; 25,116,133
LUKE 16:1-13; 41,42,46
LUKE 16:16; 6
LUKE 18:18-30; 93,133
LUKE 19:11-27; 1,47
LUKE 21:2; 1
LUKE 21:1-4; 128
LUKE 23:34; 106
LUKE 23:35; 64,65

BASIC TEXTS:
JOHN 1:19-26; 6,89
JOHN 2:13-22; 100
JOHN 6:1-15; 73-75
JOHN 12:1-13; 137

142

RELATED TEXTS:
JOHN 1:1-3; 68,89,101
JOHN 1:1-5, 10; 101
JOHN 1:10,12,16; 89
JOHN 1:19-23; 6
JOHN 1:36-42; 17,18
JOHN 1:45-51; 2
JOHN 2:13-22: 100-102
JOHN 3:1-10; 88
JOHN 3:1-21; 3
JOHN 3:16; 71
JOHN 3:16,17; 64
JOHN 6:25-71; 76
JOHN 7:1-9; 2
JOHN 7:49; 65
JOHN 11:1-45; 138,139
JOHN 14:6; 81
JOHN 15:1-17; 96,97
JOHN 17:13; ix
JOHN 18:33-42; 2
JOHN 19:15-22; 2,137
JOHN 19:15, 19 137
JOHN 19:38-42; 1
JOHN 19:39; 38
JOHN 20:24-29; 124

ACTS 1:23-26; 90
ACTS 4:32-35; 123
ACTS 4:32; 32
ACTS 4:32,34; 43,92,123
ACTS 5:1-5; 26
ACTS 5:1-11; 32
ACTS 9:1-19; 128
ACTS 9:13-18; 26
ACTS 17:6; 15
ACTS 18:1-4; 130
ACTS 22:3; 139
ACTS 23:6; 128
ACTS 24:1; 26

ROMANS 3:12; 89
ROMANS 6:5-12; 140
ROMANS 12:2; 14

I COR. 4:1; 60,61,107
I COR. 4:5; 70
I COR. 4:10; 37
I COR. 5:1,2; 37
I COR, 11:17-34; 107
I COR. 13:1-13; 107

2 COR. 5:17; 133,140
2 COR. 8:1-5; 129
2 COR. 8:2-4; 31
2 COR. 8:9; 37-39
2 COR. 8:9-14; 122
2 COR. 9:2,7,8; 107,108
2 COR. 11:17-34; 37
2 COR. 12:7-10; 37

GALATIANS 1:6-9; 37,60
GALATIANS 5:22-23; 129

EPHESIANS 2:4-10; 92,125
EPHESIANS 3:1-3; 60
EPHESIANS 5:5; 40
EPHESIANS 6:9-10; 63

PHILIPPIANS 2:6-8; 2
PHILIPPIANS 4:11-12; 39
PHILIPPIANS 4:11-19; 36,37
PHILIPPIANS 4:15-20; 130

COLOSSIANS 4:9; 27

I THESS. 5:1-11; 30

2 THESS. 3:1-13; 30

1 TIMOTHY 1:15; 37
I TIMOTHY 6:10; ix
I TIMOTHY 6:10-12; 14
1 TIMOTHY 6:17-19; 32,90

PHILEMON 1-25; 26,27

HEBREWS 4:15; 11
HEBREWS 8:1-13; 21

JAMES 2:1-8; 32

1 PETER 4:10; 9,60

2 PETER 1:16-18; 80

1 JOHN 4:16-20; 20

REVELATIONS 12:1-5; 140
REVELATIONS 12:1-17; 13
REVELATIONS 19:16; 139
REVELATIONS 21:21; 1

OLD TESTAMENT

GENESIS 2:11-12; 1
GENESIS 2:17; 80
GENESIS 13:2; 21
GENESIS 17:1-2; 21
GENESIS 27:1-32:32; 2
GENESIS 39:1-41; 84

EXODUS 20:2-17; 40,41
EXODUS 30:23-38; 1
EXODUS 35:4-9; 107
EXODUS 36:1-7; 107

LEVITICUS 6:4,5; 133
LEVITICUS 19:1-36; 6

I KINGS 9:10-14; 1

2 KINGS 18:14; 1

PSALM 69:9; 102
PSALM 103:1-22; 30
PSALM 112:1-10; 21

PROVERBS 14:31; 31

ECCLESIASTES 1:1,12; 36
ECCLESIASTES 2:1-11; 35,39
ECCLESIASTES 9:1,12; 36

ISAIAH 29:18-19; 8
ISAIAH 56:7; 101

EZEKIEL 34:1-31; 31

JEREMIAH 7:11; 101

LAMENTATIONS 3:22-23; 95

BIBLE STUDIES

General Information

As indicated in the Introduction, each chapter is brief and each chapter is distinctively different from other portions of this book. These facts open the door to at least two different kinds of Bible studies. *(P. VIII)*

A single chapter can provide the basis for a devotional. A chapter which you consider appropriate and timely can be used as an opening devotional for meetings of the church council, for meetings of the Board of Finances, and for the Stewardship Board. *(INITIALLY, AS THIS BOOK WAS WRITTEN, THE CHAPTERS WERE PREPARED AS DEVOTIONALS.)*

At meetings which are devoted to Bible study, two chapters can be chosen as the basis for presentation and discussion. While it is true that each chapter is different from the others, giving attention to two chapters at the same session deepens our appreciation for our Lord's remarkable insights concerning money.

Two chapters were chosen as the basis for three studies on the following pages. Obviously, this pattern can be used for additional Bible studies.

This approach allows opportunities for persons at this meeting to participate in the presentation. For instance, most of the chapters have texts for which there are parallel texts in the other Gospels. Inviting participants to read these texts and/or other related texts throughout the Bible can strengthen the presentation.

Portions of the Introduction can be used to begin these Bible studies. The conundrum shared by Lewis Lapham; the fact which prompted the writing of this book; and the three opportunities which it provides to the readers, may be useful way to begin a study. The leaders own experiences and insights are always appropriate. *(P. VII / P. VIII-IX)*

Chapter 23, *Money and the Lost Son,* introduces a new ministry for congregational consideration. This chapter by itself may bring forth many questions and stimulate an extensive discussion. *(P. 116-121)*

Bible Study #1, p. 1   RELATED NOTES AND OBSERVATIONS

Chapter 1 plus Chapter 15
Gold for Our King   P. 1-5

Welcome — This may be the first time that persons present have attended a Bible study with a focus on money. It may also be the first time the leader has prepared a Bible with this monetary focus.

Opening Prayer — Introduction

1. Ch. 1, title, key verse from Matthew 2:11
A quick, fun quiz. "We Three Kings of Orient Are"
> Do we know how many Wise Men there were?
> Were they kings? Did they ride on camels?
> Does your Christmas creche include the Wise Men? Did they arrive at Christmas?

    INTRODUCTION — THE FACT THAT PROMPTED THE WRITING OF THIS BOOK MAY BE USED. P. VII

2. Focusing on the gift of gold for our new born king.

    THE LEADER MAY SUMMARIZE THE INFORMATION ON P. 1 TO THE MIDDLE OF P. 2.

3. Gathering the disciples, the story of Nathaniel
The humor of Jesus.

    BOTTOM OF P. 2

4. An emphasis on Philippians 2:6-8

    THE LEADER MAY WANT TO HAVE THESE VERSES READ IN UNISON BY EVERYONE.

5. Our King before Pilate; his crucifixion and burial.

    P. 3

6. A summary of our King's journey.

    BOTTOM PARAGRAPH, P. 3

7. Gold against the background of the climax of Handel's *Messiah*.

    P. 4

> *King of Kings and Lord of Lords*
> *And He shall reign for ever and ever.*
> *Hallelujah! Hallelujah! Hallelujah!*

Gold is seen as of secondary importance, scarcely worth mentioning at all.

8. It is suggested that you move immediately to ch. 15.
    > In ch. 1 the focus was on gold and on our King.
    > In ch. 15, the focus is on silver and on a multitude of men, women, and children; on people like us.

    SEE THE FOLLOWING PAGE.

Bible Study #1, p. 2

RELATED NOTES AND OBSERVATIONS

Chapter 1 plus Chapter 15
Listening at the Edges

P. 73-77

9. Ch. 15, title, key verse, John 6:6
This key verse does not readily bring to mind the miracle of the feeding of the 5,000. This story is recorded in all four Gospels. Details from all four Gospels will be noted in sharing this story.

P. 73

10. Our focus on money prompts us to note the personal conversation Jesus had with Philip.

BOTTOM PARAGRAPH, P. 73 PLUS TOP THREE PARAGRAPHS, P. 74

11. The meaning of miracles

4TH PARAGRAPH, P. 74

12. Listening to the offer of the young boy. The leader may want to underscore the importance of his sacrifice.

BOTTOM PARAGRAPH, P. 74
TOP PARAGRAPH, P. 75

13. The miracle of feeding all those people with the meal of a young boy. What happened to all the silver coins which the disciples stewed about? To be answered later.

MIDDLE OF P. 75

14. *Listening at the Edges* by considering the context of this story. It is followed by the miracle of Jesus walking on the Sea of Galilee.

THIS IS ANOTHER MIRACLE AS A SIGN OF HIS DIETY.

15. Then he chose to teach his disciples about *living bread*. Now we are invited to his feast that we know as Holy Communion.

JOHN 6:51

16. Many people were offended and stopped following Jesus. Peter spoke in behalf of the 12 and of us as to why we will continue to follow him.

JOHN 6:54-57

JOHN 6:66

17. In this context we ask what happened to all that silver? The coins never left the possession of the disciples.

18. Against the background of our Lord's compassion for us as shown in Holy Communion, we now see the silver coins as of secondary importance, scarcely worth mentioning at all.

COMMENTS. QUESTIONS, AND FURTHER DISCUSSION WILL BE ENCOURAGED.

Bible Study #2, p. 1

RELATED NOTES AND OBSERVATIONS

Chapter 4 plus Chapter 19
Money and the Making of Disciples

P. 15-19

Welcome — You may want to commend the persons present for their courage in participating in another Bible study with a focus on money. Actually, these are double barreled sessions for two chapters will be the focus for each of these studies.

Opening Prayer — Introduction
You may choose to introduce this session with the questions found in the Introduction. Persons present may feel that those questions do not apply to them for they are "middle class" Americans. They are right. However, note the bottom paragraphs in the related column on pages 20 and 22. In the 1st century people saw themselves as either poor or rich. The disciples saw themselves a rich; middle class Americans are rich.

P. VII, TOWARD TOP OF PAGE

THESE PARAGRAPHS DEAL WITH THE TERM *MIDDLE CLASS*.

1. Monetary considerations prompt us to search for meaning.

P. 15, FIRST FOUR PARAGRAPHS. SUMMARIZE IN YOUR OWN WORDS.

2. The story of money and the making of disciples.

P. 16, SUMMARIZE IN YOUR OWN WORDS.

3. Peter's personal encounter with Jesus.

P. 17, FIRST THREE PARAGRAPHS.

4. Interpreting *immediately* and *everything*.

BOTTOM HALF OF P. 17 PLUS P. 18.

5. Following along in the footsteps of the disciples, we will discover what they learned about money and its proper place in the kind of fishing they will practice.

Before moving to chapter 19, you may pause to consider what Jesus had to say about rich persons like the disciples and like us. Jesus said, *"It is easier for a camel to go through the eye of a needle than for a rich persons to enter the kingdom of God." When the disciples heard this they were greatly astounded and said, "Then who can be saved?" But Jesus looked at them and said, "For mortals it is impossible, but for God all things are possible."*

MATTHEW 19:24-26

With this sober proclamation, it is time to move on to chapter 19.

Bible Study #2, p. 2   RELATED NOTES AND OBSERVATIONS

Chapter 4 plus Chapter 19
Generosity: His and Ours

6. Title, key verse, Matthew 20:15. Listening to this key verse readily brings to mind this astonishing and familiar parable.

    P. 95-98

7. A review of this parable and its purpose.

    P. 95, FIRST 6 PARAGRAPHS. SUMMARIZE IN YOUR OWN WORDS.

8. Using our imagination as to what might have happened on the following days and years.

    P. 95, BOTTOM PARAGRAPH TO TOP HALF OF P. 96

9. Does this extraordinary parable merit our serious attention?

    P. 96, PARAGRAPHS 4.

10. Within our imagination, we see a pattern developing.

    P. 96, PARAGRAPHS 5 & 6.

11. Turning this parable up-side-down.

    P. 96, BOTTOM PARAGRAPH, TOP TWO PARAGRAPHS.

12. The most fascinating part of this continuing story.

    P. 96, PARAGRAPHS 4, 5, & 6.

13. As the years pass by . . .

    P. 96, BOTTOM PARAGRAPH THROUGH P. 97

14. In this present time, when the offering has been received, we often sing these words:
>Let the vineyards be fruitful, Lord,
>and fill to the brim our cup of blessing.
>Gather a harvest from the seeds that
>   were sown,
>that we may be fed with the bread of life.
>Gather the hopes and dreams of all;
>unite them with the prayers we offer.
>Grace our table with your presence,
>and give us a foretaste of the feast to come.

LET THE VINEYARDS BE FRUITFUL, LORD/ HYMN # 184 EVANGELICAL LUTHERAN WORSHIP

15. It is now time for the comments, questions, and concerns of the persons present. In consideration of some questions or concerns, the group itself may be encouraged to participate in the discussion.

Bible Study #3, p. 1   RELATED NOTES AND OBSERVATIONS

    Chapter 18 - plus - Chapter 25
Wealth: A Worrisome Wonder   P. 88-94

Welcome - At this session, we will focus on giving, our giving. This is a sensitive topic for many people. From their point of view, money - especially the giving of their money - is the sum and substance of stewardship. In this session we want to share a more complete picture of stewardship as revealed through the teachings of Jesus.

Opening Prayer - Introduction
    You may choose to introduce this session by quoting the 3rd and 4th paragraphs in the Introduction, including the quotation from Lewis Lapham's book, *Money and Class In America, Notes and Observations on our Civil Religion.*   P. VII

    From our perspective, this paradox seems so unbelievable we may have difficulty talking it seriously. If our yearly income was in 6, or 7 figures, is it possible that we could feel poor? During this session, we will consider two chapters: *Wealth: A Worrisome Wonder* and *Pharisee / Tax Collector / Tithing.*

1. Ch. 18, 2 stories; first, the story of a rich young man; second, our story as person's of wealth. For both stories, the key verse is Jesus' words: *Truly, I tell you, it will be hard for a rich person to enter the kingdom of God.*
2. The first story is told on p. 88-90. You are encouraged to tell this story in your words rather than reading it off the pages. The first paragraph at the top of p. 90 refers to two words, *the money,* which are not in the Greek text. You may prefer to omit this detail in telling these stories.   THESE WORDS ARE NOT FOUND IN THE RSV, KJV, OR OTHER TRANSLATIONS.
3. The second story is told on p. 91-93.
4. In Chapter 24, *Rich Man, Poor Man,* are some facts which may help your group to measure their wealth against the background of riches and poverty.   P. 122-125

Move on to chapter 25. Assure the group there will be time for discussion following this presentation.

Bible Study #3, p. 2

RELATED NOTES AND OBSERVATIONS

> Chapter 18 - plus - Chapter 25
> *Pharisee / Tax Collector / Tithing*   P. 127-130

5. We are now confronted by a story which is very different from the stories we have just told. This story is a parable which is found in Luke, chapter 18. We will look at that parable from the perspective of tithing.
6. The story of this parable is told on p. 127 to the top paragraph on p. 128. Again, your summary of this material is more memorable than reading these paragraphs.
7. The 2nd and 3rd paragraphs remind us that Saul/Paul was a Pharisee and that Matthew was a tax collector.

8. The remainder of this chapter is about tithing. Note the primary emphasis about tithing . . . *justice, mercy and faith* or *justice and the love of God.*
9. Note also the paragraphs from the Sermon on the Mount.

10. You may want to summarize all or a portion of the paragraphs in the rest of this chapter.

Many things have been mentioned during this session. You may want to take them back to one issue, inviting their comments and questions, and then move on to other important issues for their reactions.

YOU MAY DECIDE TO BEGIN THE DISCUSSION WITH THE PARADOX FOUND ON P. VII

The leader does not have to be the only person who gives answers to questions or who comments on the comments from the group. A group discussion of these issues provides a memorable experience for participants.

YOU MAY WANT TO LIST THE ISSUES ON A BLACKBOARD, AND ASKING IF THERE ARE ADDITIONAL ISSUES THEY WANT TO DISCUSS.

These three Bible studies have focused on six of the 27 chapters in this book. Other presentations can be given to various groups within the congregation. Jesus' teachings about money merit our attention.

JESUS' TEACHINGS ABOUT MONEY
BASIC REFERENCE BOOKS

Metzger, Bruce M. and Murphy, Roland E., editors
    New Revised Standard Version, 1989
        The New Oxford Annotated Bible
        Oxford University Press, New York, 1994

May, Herbert G. and Metzger, Bruce M., editors
    Revised Standard Version, 1952
        The New Oxford Annotated Bible
        Oxford University Press, New York, 1977

Jones, Alexander, general editor
    The Jerusalem Bible (translation by Roman Catholic scholars in Jerusalem, 1966)
        Doubleday & Co. Inc., Garden City, NY, 1968

Sandmel, Samuel, general editor
    The New English Bible (translation by British scholars for British readers, 1970)
        Oxford Study Edition
        Oxford University Press, New York, 1976

    Holy Bible —King James Version (translation by British scholars, 1611)
        Camex International, NY, 1984

Douglas, J. D, organizing editor
    The New Bible Dictionary
        Wm B. Eerdmans Publishing Co., Grand Rapids, MI, 1973

Richardson, Alan, editor
    A Theological Word Book of the Bible
        The Macmillan Co., NY, 1951

    The Interpreter's Bible
        Abingdon Press, Nashville, TN, 1986

BIBLIOGRAPHY

Aland, Kurt, editor
> *Synopsis of the Four Gospels*
> *Greek-English Edition*
>> Wurttemberg Bibelanstalt Stuttgart/West Germany, 1976

Auden, W. H.
> *The Collected Works of W. H. Auden*
>> Random House, New York, 1945

Bainton, Roland
> *Here I Stand*
> *A Life of Martin Luther*
>> Abingtdon-Cokesburgy, New York, 1950

Beckman, David M.
> *Where Faith and Economics Meet — A Moral Assessment*
>> Augsburg, Minneapolis, 1981

Birch, Bruce C. and Rasmussen, Larry L.
> *The Predicament of the Prosperous*
>> Augsburg, Minneapolis, 1978

Billington, James H.
> *Russia, In Search for Itself*
>> Woodrow Wilson Center Press, Washington, DC, 2004

Dickens, Charles
> *The Christmas Carol*
>> Bantom, New York, 1995 (originally published in 1843)

Drucker, Peter F.
> *Post-Capitalist Society*
>> HarperBusiness, New York, 1993

Dungan, Nathan
> *Prodigal Sons & Material Girls*
>> Jon Wiley & Sons, Inc., Hoboken, NJ, 2003

Easterbrook, Gregg
> *The Progress Paradox*
> *How Life Gets Better While People Feel Worse*
>> Random House, New York, 2003

Ehrenreich, Barbara
> *Nickled and Dimed*
>> Metropolitan, New York, 2001

Foster, Richard J.
> *Freedom of Simplicity*
>> HarperSanFrancisco, 1981

Friedman, Thomas L.
> *The World Is Flat — A Brief History of the 21st Century*
>> Farrar, Straus, and Giroux, New York, 2005

Fretheim, Terence E.
> *About the Bible — Short Answers to Big Questions*
>> Augsburg, Minneapolis, 1999

Galbraith, John Kenneth
> *The Affluent Society*
>> New American Library, New York, 1984

Golv, John L.
> *Our Stewardship — Managing Our Assets*
>> Augsburg Fortress, Minneapolis, 2002

Hall, Douglas John
> *The Steward — A Biblical Symbol Come of Age*
>> Friendship Press, New York, 1982

Hawkin, Paul
> *The Ecology of Commerce — A Declaration of Sustainability*
>> HarperBusiness, New York, 1993

Heilbroner, Robert
> *21st Century Capitalism*
>> W. W. Norton & Co., New York, 1993

Hong, Edna
> *The Downward Ascent*
>> Augsburg Publishing, Minneapolis, 1979

Jackson, Kevin, edited by
> *The Oxford Book of Money*
>> Oxford University Press, New York, 1996

Kantonen, T. A.
> *A Theology for Christian Stewardship*
>> Wits and Stock, Eugene, OR, 2001

Klobuchar, Jim and Wilkes, Susan Cornell
> *The Miracles of Barefoot Capitalism*
>> Kirk House Publishers, Minneapolis, 2003

Lapham, Lewis W.
> *Money and Class in America*
> *Notes and Observations on our Civil Religion*
>> Weidenfeld & Nicholson, New York, 1988

Lindsey, Brink
> *The Age of Abundance*
>> HarperCollins Publishers, New York, 2007

Luther, Martin
> *The Small Catechism*
> *In Contemporary English*
>> Augsburg Publishing House, Minneapolis, 1960

Lewis, C.S.
> *The Great Divorce*
>> McMillan Co., 1946

Maier, Paul L.
> *More Than A Skeleton*
>> Thomas Nelson, Publishers, Nashville, 2003

Meeks, M. Douglas
> *God the Economist*
> *The Doctrine of God and Political Economy*
>> Fortress Press, Minneapolis, 1989

Miles, Jack
> *Christ — A Crisis in the Life of God*
>> Alfred A. Knopf, New York, 2001

Moore, Carl H. and Russell, Alvin E.
> *Money: Its Origin, Development, and Modern Use*
>> McFarland Publishing, NC, 1987

Moore, Gary
> *Ten Golden Rules for Financial Success*
> *Riches I Have Gathered from Legendary Sir John W. Templeton*
> > Zonderman Publishing House, Grand Rapids, MI, 1996

Needleman, Jacob
> *Money and the Meaning of Life*
> > Doubleday, New York, 1991

Novak, Michael
> *Business as a Calling — Work and the Examined Life*
> > The Free Press, New York, 1996

Pilgrim, Walter E.
> *Good News to the Poor*
> *Wealth and Poverty in Luke-Acts*
> > Augsburg Publishing House, Minneapolis, 1983

Potok, Chaim
> *Wanderings*
> *History of the Jews*
> > Alfred A. Knopf, New York, 1978

Samuelson, P.A.
> *Economics: An Introductory Analysis*
> > McGraw Hill, New York, 1948

Samuelson, P.A. and Nordhaus, William
> *Economics*
> > Irwin/McGraw Hill, Boston, 1998

Schumacher, E. F.
> *Small Is Beautiful — Economics as if People Mattered*
> > Harper and Row, New York, 1973

Skibbe, Eugene M.
> *A Quiet Reformer*
> *From a Gospel Voice in Nazi Germany to a New Vision of Christian Unity*
> > Kirk House Publishing, Minneapolis, MN 1999

Stackhouse, Max L.
> *Public Theology and Political Economy —*
> *Christian Stewardship in Modern Society*
> > Eerdmans, Grand Rapids, MI, 1987

Thurow, Lester C.
> *The Future of Capitalism*
>> William Morrow & Co., Inc., New York, 1986

Waldman, Michael
> *My Fellow Americans,*
> *The Most Important Speeches by American Presidents*
>> Sourcebooks, Inc., Naperville, IL, 2003

INDEX

A Life of Martin Luther
   (Bainton), 43
A Quiet Reformer
   (Skibbe), 69
A Theology for Christian Stewardship,
   (Kantonen), 59-60
Abraham: A Journey to the Heart of Three Faiths, (Feiler), 28
Age of Abundance, The
   (Lindsey), 118
Auden, W. H.
   Collected Poetry of, 52-53

Bainton, Roland
   A Life of Martin Luther, 43
Billington, James H.
   Russia in Search of Itself, 113

Christ: A Crisis in the Life of God,
   (Miles), 88
Christmas Carol, The
   (Dickens), 42, 48
Collected Poetry of W. H. Auden,
   (Auden), 52-53
Commerce
   business men and women, viii, 40
   finances, viii
Congregation
   lay leaders, viii, ix,
   ministries, ix
   parish pastors, viii, ix
   workers within, 95-98
Contentment,
   Paul, 36-38

Dante
   Divine Comedy, 54-55
Dickens, Charles
   Christmas Carol, The, 48
Disciples,
   first mission, 52-65
   immediately and *everything,* 17-18
   making of, 15-18

Divine Comedy
   (Dante), 54-55
Downward Ascent, The
   (Hong), 80
Drucker, Peter F.
   Post-Capitalist Society, 7, 8
   a transition period, 32-33, 86
   knowledge and service workers, 48
   pension funds, 48
Dungan, Nathan
   Prodigal Sons and Material Girls
   118-119

Easterbook, Glenn
   The Progress Paradox, 124
Economics
   (Samuelson and Nordhaus), 124
Economics: An Introductory Analysis
   (Samuelson), 124
Ehrenreich, Barbara
   Nickel and Dimed, 124

Feiler, Bruce
   Abraham: A Journey to the Heart of Three Faiths, 28
Financial Success
   (Moore), 58
Foster, Richard J.
   Freedom of Simplicity, 43
Friedman, Thomas L.
   World Is Flat, The, 118
Future of Capitalism, The
   (Thurow), 13

God the Economist
   (Meeks), 41, 59
God Incarnate
   bread into living bread, 76
   walking on the sea, 75
   water into wine, 75
Golv, John L.
   Our Stewardship; Managing Our Assets, 91, 102

Hawkin, Paul
   The Ecology of Commerce, 27

Heilbroner, Robert
   21st Century Capitalism, 23, 48
History
   first century, 21, 22
Hong, Edna
   Downward Ascent, The, 80
Humor
   Nathaniel, 2
   parable of the Sower, 67-69
   worrying, 53
Hymns
   Beautiful Savior, ELW, #838, 140
   Here I Am, Lord, ELW, #574, 134-135
Hyperbole, 27-28

Introduction to the Synoptic Gospels
   (Jerusalem Bible), 79

Jerusalem Bible
   Introduction to the Synoptic Gospels, 79
Jesus
   divinity of, 3, 75
   humanity of, 11-13
   humor of, 2, 3, 67, 68
   hyperbole of, 127-128
   kingship, 3
John the Baptist
   our forerunner, 6, 8, 9
   repentance, 6, 7

Kantonen, T. A.
   A Theology for Christian Stewardship
      59-60
King
   King Herod, 2, 3
   King of Israel, 2-4
   magi (wise men), 1
Kingdom of God
   forgiveness, 83-86
   mission statement, 62
   riches, 20
   worry, 52
Klobuchar, Jim
   Miracles of Barefoot Economics, The, 125
Klobuchar and Wilkes
   Miracles of Barefoot Economics, The, 125

Lapham, Lewis H.
   Money and Class in America, vii, 23, 86
Lazarus
   the rich man, and, 122, 123
Linchpin
   commercial enterprises, 46-50
   Gospel ministries, 40-44
   greed, 46
   talents, 47-48
Luther, Martin
   coin in the coffer, 43
   Small Catechism, The, 93
Lutheran Social Services, 44

Maier, Paul I.
   More Than a Skeleton, 116
Meeks, M. Douglas
   God the Economist
   financial language, 59
   idolatry, 41
Middle Class, vii, 20
Miles, Jack
   Christ: A Crisis in the Life of God, 88
Miracles
   feeding of the 5000, 73-76
   meaning of, 74
   walking on the sea, 75
   water into wine, 75
Miracles of Barefoot Capitalism, The
   (Klobuchar and Wilkes), 125
Money
   costly perfume, 137-139
   counting the cost, 110-114
   denarii (silver), 1, 42, 75
   gold, 1, 2, 4, 64
   good usages of, 434-44
   history of, 57-59
   Jewish *Lepton,* 1, 128
   language of, 78-81
   linchpin, 40-50
   making of disciples, 15-18
   mercy and justice, 133-135
   ministry without money, 62-65
   power of, 83-86
   prayer, house of, 100-103

Money (continued
   reconciliation, 24, 26
   robbers, 100-103
   Roman *denarii,* (silver), 1, 62, 73, 138
   sad usages of, 42, 43
   scarcity of, vii
   secondary importance, 4, 13, 81, 103, 138
   surplus of, vii
   talents, 84
   taxes, 105-108
   temptations, 11-13
   tithing, 127-130
   treasures in heaven, 35.38
   two worlds, 15-18
   worldly cares, 67-68
Money and Class in America
   (Lapham), vii, 23, 86
Money; It's Origin, Development and Modern Use, (Moore), 57-58
Moore, Carl H. and Russell, Alvin E.
   Money; It's Origin, Development and Modern Use, 57-58
Moore, Gary
   Financial Success, 58
Motto of our nation
   In God We Trust, 13
My Fellow Americans
   (Waldman), 52

Needleman, Jacob
   Money and the Meaning of Life
   time-poor society, 23
   two worlds, 15-17
New Oxford Annotated Bible
   The Gospels, *Their Literary Genre,* viii, ix
   proclamation, 101, 103
Nickel and Dimed
   (Ehrenreich), 124
Nordhaus, Wm.
   Economics, 124
Novak, Michael
   Business as a Calling, 40

Our Stewardship; Managing Our Assets
   (Golv), 91, 102

Parables
   interpretations, 67
   Dishonest Manager, 41-42
   Elder Brother, 25, 116
   Good Samaritan, 110-113
   Laborers in the Vineyard, 95-96
   Mustard Seed, p. 70
   Pharisee and the Tax Collector, 127-128
   Prodigal Son, 116-118
   Rich Man and Lazarus, 122-124
   Sower and Seed, 67-69
   The Talents, 45-47
   The Yeast, 70
   Weeds and Wheat, 69-70
Poor People
   a special place, 30-33
   Rich man and Lazarus, 122-123
   why a special place?, 30-33
Post-Capitalist Society
   (Drucker), 7, 8, 32, 33, 48, 86
Poverty. vii
   financial, 47
   measuring our, 124
   privileges, 85
   spiritual, 20
Prodigal Sons and Material / Girls
   (Dungan), 118-119
Progress Paradox, The
   (Easterbook), 124

Reconciliation
   Ananias / Saul / Paul, 25-26
   elder brother, 25
   hospitality, 65
   Onesimus, 26-27
Rich People
   privileges, 86
   talents, 47-50
   10,000 talents, 84
Russell, Alvin E.
   Money, It's Origin, Development, and Modern Use, 57-58
Russia in Search of Itself
   (Billington), 113

Skibbe, Eugene M.
   A Quiet Reformer, 69
Samuelson, P. A.
   Economics: An Introductory Analysis, 124
Samuelson, P.A. and Nordhaus, Wm.
   Economics, 124
Small Catechism, The
   (Luther), 93
Stewardship, 59-60

Teachings about Money
   economics and the kingdom, 52-60
   miracles, 74
   parables, 67
   poverty, 122-125
   proclamation, 101
   reconciliation, 25-28
   redemption, 116-117
   wealth, 122-125
Temptations
   of Jesus, 11-13
   ours, 11-13
Thurow, Lester
   Future of Capitalism, The, 13
Tithing
   practice of, 128-130
Treasures
   contentment, 36-37
   on earth, in heaven, 35-38
   Solomon, 35-36

Volunteerism
   civil religion, 33
   non-profit organizations, 7

Waldman, Michael
   My Fellow Americans, 52
Wealth, vii, 20, 21
   generosity, 95-98
   measuring our, 124-125
   worries about, 88-93
Wealthy Men, 88
Wealthy Women, 88, 122
*World Is Flat, The — A Brief History of the
   21st Century,* (Friedman), 118

Wilkes, Susan Cornell
   Miracles of Barefoot Capitalism, 125

Zacchaeus, 129, 132, 133